KNITS for BEARS to WEAR

KNITS *for* BEARS *to* WEAR

MORE THAN 20 FUN, KNIT-TO-FIT FASHIONS

for all teddies and toys including 18-inch dolls

Amy O'Neill Houck

Potter
CRAFT

NEW YORK

Published in the United States by Potter Craft, an imprint of the Crown Publishing

Group, a division of Random House, Inc., New York.

www.pottercraft.com

POTTER CRAFT and colophon is a registered trademark of Random House, Inc.

Library of Congress Cataloging-in-Publication Data is available upon request.

ISBN 978-0-307-40661-3

Printed in China

Design by Amy Sly
Photographs by Ted Tuel
Illustrations by Kristi Porter

Thanks to the Craft Yarn Council of America (www.yarnstandards.com) for their
Standard Yarn Weights System Chart, which appears on page 95.

1 3 5 7 9 10 8 6 4 2

First Edition

Table of Contents

Introduction

Since you've stopped to read this introduction before diving right into the myriad fun and fancy outfits for your furry friends, I'll let you in on a secret: This book is more than just a book of clothes for toys. Quite frankly, I had an ulterior motive when I accepted the challenge of creating more than twenty designs for teddy bears. I love designing in teddy-bear scale. Sophisticated clothes made in tiny proportions allow for creative exploration without the huge commitment of an adult-sized garment.

When I teach a knitting workshop, I often have my students prepare a miniature version of a project so they can finish every technique in the syllabus in one sitting. Of course, while my students go home with one tiny sock or a teeny sweater as a memento of their class, in making the patterns from this book you'll get more—a treasured gift for a young friend or a new piece for your own bear or doll's wardrobe. These projects are small and portable, and many work up in an evening or two. That's why I've included a wide range of techniques and garment constructions for you to explore in the pages to come. You can try seamless top-down knitting, work a T-shirt sideways, or get a step-by-step introduction to set-in sleeves. You can knit a pair of jeans, try your hand at mosaic knitting, lace, and more.

Here's another secret: All of the patterns in this book are scalable. I've set up the patterns using an easy-to-follow format that allows you to create your projects for any sized doll or bear. This means no matter what size toy you want to dress, you'll get a perfect fit. In fact, if you really wanted, you could knit a matching garment for the bear's owner!

We'll begin by showing you how to measure your bear, and you'll use those measurements as you make the patterns. I've even included a chart on page 9 where you can keep track of your bear fittings. The format also allows you to easily change yarn, needle size, and even stitch pattern. My hope is that, as you work each pattern, you'll gain the confidence and inspiration to develop your own creations.

MEET THE BEARS

Pearl, Eddie, and Joey were my muses and models for the projects in this book. They were chosen after a rigorous elimination process, too grueling for reality television. They are classic teddies, in the most common bear size range (16–18" [40.5–45.5cm] tall). Luckily, they also have great fashion sense, so they were a joy to design for.

Pearl loves to be frilly and girly, but she has a hipper side as well. She favors pink and purple. She loves to dress to the nines and play dress-up.

Pearl's brother, Eddie, is more of a casual dresser. He loves to relax and hang out. He's a sweater and jeans kind of guy, and he doesn't like to fuss about his clothes.

Joey is Eddie's best friend, but they couldn't be more different. Joey is always busy. He could be stirring up potions or making honey buns, running on the basketball court or hiking in the woods—and he's always perfectly dressed for the occasion.

Getting Started

Before beginning a project, it's important to learn how to use the patterns featured here and how to measure your bear to get a perfect fit. In this section, I also describe all the special techniques and tools you'll need for the projects in the book.

MEASURING YOUR TOY

Like every person, every bear or doll is different. Even if your toy is 16–18" (40.5–45.5cm) tall like Pearl, Eddie, and Joey, it may have a bigger head, shorter arms or torso, or in the case of Pearl and Eddie, unusually wide hips. Keep in mind also that dolls of the same height may be thinner than bears. So to begin any project, you need to measure your toy. Some standard measurements are listed in the chart below. (Project-specific measurements will be noted throughout the book.) You can make notes about your bear right here in the book, or if you're knitting for many toys, make copies of this chart to keep track of all the measurements.

HOW TO MEASURE

Use a dressmaker's measuring tape, and be sure to measure from "point to point." For example, if you're measuring from head to toe, find the tallest part of the head and measure down to the very bottom of the foot. If you're measuring a width or circumference, be sure to take the measurement at the widest part of your bear.

HOW TO USE THE PATTERNS

All of the patterns in the book are sized for 16–18" (40.5–45.5cm) bears. If you want to knit for a toy with a different height or width; tweak the gauge, yarn weight, or stitch pattern; or add your own details, you'll find the customizing sidebars a big help. They let you make every project in this book *your* project. Here's how to get started:

- Read the entire pattern to get an idea for what you'll be doing. If you notice any unfamiliar techniques, check the beginning of the pattern and the information in this chapter.

Measurement Chart

Head Circumference: _____

Neck Circumference: _____

Back Neck Width: _____

Shoulder Width (edge to edge): _____

Chest Circumference: _____

Chest Width (between the arms): _____

Belly Circumference (at the widest point): _____

Arm Length (from shoulder to paw): _____

Outer Leg Length (from outside leg join to bottom of foot): _____

Inside Leg Measurement (from inseam to foot): _____

Length (from base of neck to bottom of back): _____

- **Choose your yarn and needles.** Every yarn in this book was chosen with great care, and you'll surely enjoy using them. You can also use whatever yarn you have on hand. Tiny projects are great for stash busting. I usually recommend that when substituting yarns, knitters take a close look at the weight and yardage of the skein and find a yarn that matches closely on both counts. For example, if I used a yarn that's 100 meters per 50g, then you should find one that has a similar meters-to-grams ratio.

- **Make a generous 6" (15cm) swatch.** Of course, if you're making a tiny bear garment, a swatch of that size may seem like more knitting than you're liable to do for the garment itself. The temptation not to swatch may be strong. Just remember: *No swatching usually means more ripping and re-knitting later on.* Once you've picked the yarn for your project, knit a swatch starting with the needle size suggested in the pattern. Change needle sizes every few inches until you get the gauge specified, if necessary.

- **Block your swatch.** Put it through whatever rigors the final garment will get. If it's lace, do a wet block. If you don't think the garment will need much blocking, you should at least stretch and manipulate your swatch to even out the stitches and get a more accurate measurement.

- **Take careful measurements of your gauge** after blocking your swatch and laying it flat. Measure to two decimal places, e.g., 5.45". Don't round when you're measuring.

- **If you're using the pattern gauge** and you're knitting for the model-sized bear, you're ready to start knitting the garment. If not, it's time to have some fun with the customizing sidebar.

USING THE CUSTOMIZING SIDEBARS

- Read the entire main pattern before you start your customizing calculations. You'll have a better idea of what you're going to be doing and where you'll need to customize.

- Use your gauge and your toy measurements (and a calculator, if you'd like) to walk through the step-by-step guide in the sidebar.

- First, you'll figure out how many stitches to cast on. If you need to cast on a multiple of a particular number or an even or odd number, the sidebar specifies how to round to that number. Unless you're using very bulky yarn, it won't affect sizing too much to round your stitch count up or down—I suggest rounding up unless the pattern says otherwise.

- Often, a sidebar will refer back to the main pattern for a while, then ask you to do another calculation or make an adjustment. At these points, it makes sense to use a sticky note to mark the spot in the main pattern where you should look back to the customizing sidebar, so you don't lose your place. This is just another reason you should read through the pattern before you begin knitting.

ON CHARTS AND SCHEMATICS

For most projects, I've included detailed schematics of the size and shape of the project. Schematics can be a great help for blocking—you can use the measurements as a guide. They can also be helpful when you're making changes to a project. The visual guide will allow you to imagine and make note of what you want to do differently. If you're changing stitch patterns, you might find it useful to knit to the measurements listed on the schematic instead of a row count or stitch count given in the pattern.

For patterns that include lace or colorwork, you'll find stitch charts. If you're a visual learner, you may find it much easier to read the stitch chart than to read the word-by-word instructions for lace. Every chart in this book begins on a right-side row. The Right Side is read from right to left (like your knitting) and the Wrong Side is read from left to right (as if the Right Side were always facing you). A knit symbol on the Right Side is represented the same way as a purl symbol on the Wrong Side. Each chart includes a key for the symbols it contains.

SPECIAL KNITTING TECHNIQUES

Special stitch patterns related to a specific project and special abbreviations are always described at the beginning of the project itself. There are, however, a few techniques I want to draw particular attention to that you may not find in your standard how-to-knit book.

I-Cord

To make a knitted cord, use one circular or two double-pointed needles. Cast on the number of stitches specified in the pattern. *Knit one row. Do not turn your work. Instead, keeping the side you just worked facing you, slide the stitches to the opposite point of the needle. Carry the yarn across the back of the work, and knit one row. Repeat from * until the I-cord is the length specified in the pattern.

Provisional Cast-On Techniques

For several of the projects, including the Blue Jeans (page 39), Drop-Stitch Skirt (page 19), and Traveling Vines Sundress (page 25), I suggest a provisional cast-on to begin the project. There are many ways to work a provisional cast-on. Perhaps the easiest is with a crocheted chain.

Crocheted Chain Cast-On

STEP 1 With a crochet hook slightly larger than your needle size, crochet a chain 3 or 4 stitches longer than the number of stitches needed to cast on. (See the crochet instructions on page 13 if you need help making a chain.)

STEP 2 Flip the chain to its backside, so you can see the little bumps running up the middle of the Vs that make up the chain.

STEP 3 Insert your knitting needle into the second bump and draw up a loop. Continue along the chain, picking up the required number of stitches through the chain bumps. Later, when you're ready to use the provisional stitches, unravel the chain, and slide what are now the live stitches onto a needle one by one.

Updated Invisible Cast-On

Elizabeth Zimmermann called this the Invisible Cast-On. It's my favorite provisional cast-on because it's fast and easy. Instead of waste yarn, I use a spare circular needle. That way, when you're ready to knit the provisional stitches, they're already on a needle and ready to go.

STEP 1 Make a slipknot with the main project yarn. Slide it over a spare circular needle and onto the cable.

STEP 2 Hold the cable of the circular needle with your thumb and the yarn over your index finger (as if you were working a long-tail cast-on).

STEP 3 With the project needle in your right hand, dip the point under the cable and up into the space between the cable and the main yarn.

STEP 4 With the needle in front of the main yarn, push a loop back under the cable and up over the project needle. (1st stitch cast on.)

STEP 5 Bring the project needle above and behind the yarn. Yarn over, bringing the yarn away from you. The needle is now in the space between the cable and the yarn. (2nd stitch cast on.)

Repeat steps 3–5 to cast on the required number of stitches. Let the spare cable hang freely until you're ready to flip your work upside down and knit the provisional stitches.

Three-Needle Bind-Off

Hold the two pieces of knit fabric to be joined parallel with their right sides together (unless the pattern specifies otherwise). *Insert a third needle through the stitches on the tips of the two left-hand needles at once, and knit those stitches together as one. Once two stitches are worked and on the right-hand needle, bind off by passing the stitch farthest from the tip over the stitch nearest to the tip. Repeat from * until you've bound off the required number of stitches.

Three-Needle Non-Bind-Off

This technique, aptly named by knitting guru Cat Bordhi, is an adaptation of a traditional three-needle bind-off. The Three-Needle Non-Bind-Off is worked the same way as the traditional Three-Needle Bind-Off, but without the binding off step. Essentially, you're joining two pieces of fabric but leaving the stitches live to be worked further. This technique is great, when combined with a provisional cast-on, for creating hems (like the Picot Hem in the Traveling Vines Sundress, page 25) or drawstring casings (like in the Drop Stitch Skirt, page 19, or Blue Jeans, page 39). I've also used it to create the henley neck opening in the Floral Nightgown (page 80) and Footie Jammies (page 85).

CROCHET TECHNIQUES

For detailed instructions on how to crochet, I recommend *Teach Yourself Visually Crochet* by Kim Werker and Cecily Keim. Here are the techniques you'll need for the projects in this book.

Crochet a Chain

Make a slip knot and slip it over the crochet hook. *Wrap the yarn around the hook and pull it through the loop on the hook (1 chain [ch] made). Repeat from * until you have the length of chain specified.

Single Crochet

Single crochet (sc) can be worked into a crocheted chain, crocheted stitches, or knit fabric. If you're crocheting into knit fabric, space the stitches evenly. If the fabric starts to pucker, you're using too few crochet stitches. If the fabric starts to flare, you're using too many.

To single crochet, *insert the hook into the stitch or fabric as specified, wrap the yarn around the hook, and pull a loop through. yarn over, and pull through both of the loops on the hook. Repeat from * for the required number of stitches.

Double Crochet

Like single crochet, double crochet (dc) can be worked into stitches of knit fabric. In the Floral Nightgown (page 80), three double crochet stitches are worked into one single crochet stitch, creating a shell motif.

To double crochet, *yarn over, insert the hook into the stitch specified, wrap the yarn around the hook, pull a loop through—3 loops on the hook. (Yarn over, pull through two loops) twice. Repeat from * for the required number of stitches.

WORKING IN SMALL CIRCLES

There are several occasions in the book where you will have the opportunity to knit tiny rounds. There are a few ways to do this.

Double-Pointed Needles

Traditionally, small rounds are worked on double-pointed needles. Divide your stitches evenly among 3 or 4 double-pointed needles. Hold one of the needles with stitches in your left hand, and an empty needle in your right. (Let the non-working needles dangle.) Knit stitches off of the first needle and onto the right-hand needle. The empty left-hand needle now becomes the new right-hand needle.

Two Circular Needles

Divide your stitches between two circular needles. Holding the needle without the working yarn in your hands, let the other needle dangle with the working yarn hanging off of the the non-working needle. Bring the yarn up, letting the needle rest, and knit across. When you've finished the first half of the round, turn the work to begin using the next circular needle.

Magic Loop

To work a small round on one long circular needle, fold the cable in half so that half of the stitches are on one side and the other half on the other. Arrange the stitches so only a few are on the tip of the working needle. The excess cable pops through the stitches as a loop and allows the small number of stitches to fit around the large needle. Often it helps to pop out two loops—one on each side. After you work the stitches on the needle tip, adjust the position of the loop to allow more stitches to slide to the tip.

TOOLS

Other than needles and yarn, there are a few tools that you'll need to create the projects in the book.

Measuring Tape

I prefer to use a flexible dressmaker's tape, the kind that retracts at the touch of a button, but any flexible measuring tape will work.

Stitch Markers

Any kind of ring can be used for a stitch marker, from the "official" markers you can buy from local yarn stores to small hair elastics. You can also use small pieces of waste yarn tied into rings as markers. Make sure the waste yarn is a color that stands out against your project yarn.

Removable Stitch Markers

A few of the projects in the book call for markers that can be removed mid-row (before you've knit the stitch they're marking). You can buy coil-less safety pins or use standard safety pins (though they sometimes catch on the yarn). You can also use waste yarn and just cut it off when you need to or, as I sometimes do, bend a plastic-coated paper clip into a ring and use it as a marker.

Straight Pins

Pins can be useful for blocking your work or for pinning pieces before sewing. Choose rust-proof pins if possible.

Scissors

If you have a pair of scissors that you use *only* for yarn, you'll find they stay sharp and do a much better job cutting fiber than paper or other craft scissors.

Calculator

None of the calculations in the book are complicated, but if it helps, by all means, use a calculator. I often do.

A Teddy Bear's Picnic

When Pearl, Eddie, and Joey get together for a day of fun, they love to play outside. A day in the sun is made even better if it includes a picnic snack. Even at playtime, Pearl likes to look her best in her hip Dropped Stitch Skirt (page 19) and Deep V Sweater (page 16) or her Ribs and Lace Cardi (page 21). The lacy Traveling Vines Sundress (page 25) is perfect for serving tea, and the Berry Bolero (page 35) is just the thing for an afternoon spent lounging in the sun. Eddie likes to keep cool in his relaxed sideways ribbed Bear-T (page 29), while Joey prefers to play in jeans and his favorite Letter Sweater (page 31), featuring a knit-purl patterned "B"—for bear, of course!

DEEP V SWEATER

What Bear doesn't want to be at the height of fashion? With a deep V-neck, wide waist ribbing, and bell sleeves, this pullover will make Pearl feel en vogue. This piece makes a great primer in top-down raglan knitting. Once you've mastered the basic techniques, you'll want to make sweaters for friends of all sizes.

Stitch Note

A note about stitch increases—this pattern has increases at the edge that will form the V-neck as well as increases along the raglan lines. Kf&b (knit into the front and back loop of the same stitch) is used for the edge increases. For the raglan increases, I used an untwisted (m1) Make One, which creates small eyelets. You can use a twisted m1 if you don't want any holes, or yarn overs if you want larger eyelets. Experiment with your swatch to see which increase you prefer.

BODY

Using size 9 (5.5mm) needles, cast on 30 stitches.

Begin the V-neck increases and set up for the raglan increases

Setup Row 1 (RS) Kf&b, place marker, k1, place marker, k6, place marker, k1, place marker, k12, place marker, k1, place marker, k6, place marker, k1, place marker, kf&b.
Setup Row 2 Purl.

Begin the raglan increases; continue the V-neck increases

Rows 1 and 3 (RS) *Knit to marker, m1, slip marker, k1, slip marker, m1, repeat from * 3 more times, knit to end.
Rows 2, 4, and 6 (WS) Purl.
Row 5 Kf&b, *knit to marker, m1, slip marker, k1, slip marker, m1, repeat from * 3 more times, knit to last stitch, kf&b.

Repeat **Rows 1–6** until the sleeves measure 7" (18cm) between the markers.

Place the sleeve stitches onto holders

Row 1 Knit to the 1st marker (working the edge increase if appropriate), place the left sleeve stitches (up to 3rd marker) on a holder, and remove the markers; cast on 2 stitches under the arm; knit across the back to the 6th marker, place the stitches for the right sleeve (up to the last marker) on a holder and remove the markers; cast on 2 stitches under the arm; knit to the end of the row (working edge increase if appropriate).

Skill Level

Easy

Finished Measurements

Chest Circumference: 16" (40.5cm)

Length: 6" (15cm)

Sleeve: 5" (13cm) from neck to cuff

Materials

1 skein Be Sweet Products Medium Mohair [100% baby mohair; 200 yd (183m) per 1¾ oz (50g)], color: buttercup, ❹

Size 9 (5.5mm) circular needles, 16" (40cm) or longer, or size needed to obtain gauge

Size 7 (4.5mm) circular needles, 16" (40cm) or longer

Size 10½ (6.5mm) circular needles, 16" (40.5cm) or longer

Measuring tape

Yarn needle

8 stitch markers

2 stitch holders

Gauge

17 stitches and 24 rows = 4" (10cm) in stockinette stitch

Pattern Note

The V-neck on this sweater is fairly deep. If you'd like a shallower neckline, work the edge decreases every third row.

You will now work on the body stitches only, continuing the edge increases as set for the V-neck until you've reached the widest part of the bear's belly.

Set up for the waist ribbing

Join to work in the round and count your stitches. Knit 1 round, decreasing as necessary to adjust your stitch count to a multiple of 4.

Waist ribbing

Switch to size 7 (4.5mm) needles. Work in k2, p2 rib for 2" (5cm) or until the ribbing reaches the top of the bear's legs.

Bind off in ribbing using size 9 (5.5mm) needles.

SLEEVES

Move the stitches for 1 sleeve to double-pointed or circular size 9 needles. Pick up and knit 2 stitches under the arm. Join to work in the round.

Note: If you prefer, you can work the sleeves flat and seam them up later. To do so,

cast on 2 stitches, work across the sleeve stitches, and then cast on 2 more stitches. Continue working back and forth on these stitches as directed.

Work 5 rounds with size 9 needles, then switch to size 10½ (6.5mm) needles. Work in stockinette stitch with larger needles until the sleeve measures 5" (10cm) from the neck edge or falls ¾ of the way down the bear's arm. Bind off as follows:

Round 1 *K1, YO, repeat from * around.
Round 2 S1, k1, psso, *(k1, bind off 1 stitch, s1, bind off 1 stitch) repeat from * until one stitch remains. Fasten off.

Repeat these instructions for the second sleeve.

FINISHING

Sew up the sleeves if you worked the sleeves flat. Close any underarm gaps. Weave in all ends.

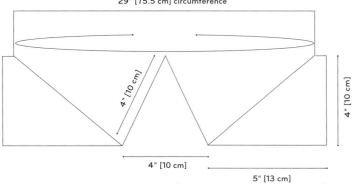

29" [75.5 cm] circumference

4" [10 cm]

4" [10 cm]

4" [10 cm]

5" [13 cm]

DROPPED STITCH SKIRT

Flirty and pink, this drop-stitch skirt has just the right amount of attitude for Pearl when she wants to be a bit "punk." The skirt begins just like the Blue Jeans (page 39), but continues without a split for the legs. I love the look of purposefully dropped stitches and I'm sure you will, too.

Skill Level

Beginner

Finished Measurements

Waist Circumference: 16" (40.5cm)

Length: 7" (18cm)

Materials

1 skein Brown Sheep Cotton Fleece [80% cotton, 20% merino wool; 215 yd (197m) per 3½ oz (100g)], color: CW240 pink-a-boo, (4) medium

Size 7 (4.5mm) circular needles, 16" (40cm) long, or size needed to obtain gauge

Spare size 7 (4.5cm) circular needle (optional)

Measuring tape

Yarn needle

Gauge

20 stitches and 28 rows = 4" (10 cm) in stockinette stitch

SKIRT

Using a provisional cast-on over a spare needle or waste yarn, (page 11), cast on 77 stitches.

Work 8 rows in stockinette stitch, ending with a WS row.

Create the Drawstring Eyelets

Next row (RS) K36, yo, ssk, k1, k2tog, yo, k36.

Work 7 rows in stockinette stitch.

WAISTBAND

Fold your knitting in half, with the wrong sides facing, and align the stitches from the provisional cast-on with the stitches on the working needle. Insert the tip of the right needle into the first stitch on the needle and the first stitch from the provisional cast-on. Knit these 2 stitches together. Repeat across. There are 77 stitches on the needle and you have formed a casing for the drawstring. Place a marker to denote the beginning of the round and join to work in the round.
Work even in stockinette stitch for 2" (5cm).

Begin the Dropped-Stitch Pattern

Round 1 *K7, place marker, yo, place marker, repeat from * around—11 stitches added.

Round 2 *Knit to 1 stitch before the first marker, k1 through the back loop, slip marker, k1, slip marker, k1 through the back loop; repeat from * around.

Round 3 Knit, but do not twist any stitches. Repeat **Rounds 2 and 3** until the skirt measures 6¾" (17cm).

Drop the Marked Stitches

Round 1 *Knit to the first marker, drop the stitch between the markers, allowing the stitch to "run" all the way down; cast on 3 stitches using the backward loop method; repeat from * around, removing the markers as you go.
Round 2 Knit.

Tip: To avoid having a "bump" in the front of the skirt, knit an extra half-round and begin the bind-off in the back of the skirt.

Bind off loosely.

FINISHING

I-Cord Drawstring

On a double-pointed or circular needle, cast on 4 stitches. Work 25" (63.5cm) of I-cord. Bind off. Thread the I-cord through the drawstring casing.

Weave in all ends.

Optional: You can choose to sew up the sides of the drawstring casing or leave it open as a tail opening for your bear.

Make a Custom-Sized Dropped Stitch Skirt

1. Measure your toy's lower body circumference at the widest point (on my bear, it's the hips, not the waist): _____ (H)

2. Note your gauge (stitches per inch/ 2.5cm): _____ (G)

3. Multiply the circumference by your gauge to determine your cast-on (CO). Adjust the number to a multiple of 7. (H) x (G) = _____ (CO)

Cast on according to your calculations and follow the instructions for the main pattern, adjusting the length of your skirt as desired for your bear.

16" [40.5 cm]
waist circumference

7" [18 cm]

19½" [49.5 cm]
hem circumference

RIBS AND LACE CARDI

Skill Level

Intermediate

Finished Measurements

Chest Circumference: 15" (38cm)

Length: 5" (12.5cm)

Sleeve: 4½" (11.5cm) From the neck to the cuff.

Materials

1 skein Malabrigo Merino Worsted [100% merino wool; 216 yd (197m) per 3½ oz (100g)], color: 60 dusty, (4) medium

Size 8 (5mm) circular needles, 24" (61cm) long, or size needed to obtain gauge

Size 5 (3.5mm) circular needles, 24" (61cm) long

Measuring tape

Yarn needle

8 stitch markers

Gauge

17 stitches and 29 rows = 4" (10cm) in stockinette stitch on larger needles

Pearl finds a cardigan is just the thing to take the chill off when she's taking a walk through the neighborhood. This lacy one, knit in luscious kettle-dyed merino, is so soft she barely knows she has it on. The sweater is knit from the top with an intuitive lace pattern at the waist and cuffs for a pretty accent.

Special Stitches

Seed Stitch

Alternate knits and purls in the first row (k1, p1), then knit the purls and purl the knits in following rows.

Tip: If worked over an odd number of stitches, rows always begin with knit.

Double Eyelet Rib (for a multiple of 7 stitches plus 2)

Row 1 (RS) *K2, p5; repeat from * to last 2 stitches, k2.

Row 2 *P2, k5; repeat from * to last 2 stitches, k2.

Row 3 Repeat Row 1.

Row 4 *P2, k2tog, yo, k1, yo, ssk; repeat from * to last 2 stitches, p2.

Repeat Rows 1–4 for pattern.

BODY

Using size 8 (5mm) needles, cast on 51 stitches.

NECK EDGE

Rows 1–3 Work in seed stitch.

Set up for the raglan increases

Row 1 (RS) K1, p1, k1 (seed stitch edge), k5, place marker k1, place marker, k8, place marker, k1, place marker, k15, place marker, k1, place marker, k8, place marker, k1, place marker, k5, k1, p1, k1.

Row 2 K1, p1, k1, purl to last 3 stitches, k1, p1, k1.

Row 3 K1, p1, k1, *knit to marker, yo, slip marker, k1, slip marker, yo, repeat from * 3 time more, knit to last 3 stitches, k1, p1, k1. Repeat **Rows 2 and 3** until the sleeve portion of the sweater measures 7" (18cm) across—measure between the increases. End with a wrong-side row.

Place the sleeve stitches on holders

On the next right-side row, k1, p1, k1, knit to the 1st marker and place stitches between the 1st and the 4th markers on a holder for the first sleeve, cast on 2 stitches for the underarm, knit across the back to the 5th marker, and place the stitches between the 5th and 8th markers on a holder for the second sleeve. Cast on 2 stitches for the underarm, knit to the last 3 stitches, k1, p1, k1.

DOUBLE EYELET RIB SETUP ROW

Count your stitches. Work in pattern, decreasing evenly across the row as needed to come to a stitch count (including the edge stitches) equal to a multiple of 7 plus 2.

Begin the Double Eyelet Rib

Switch to size 5 (3.5mm) needles.

Continue to work the 3 edge stitches on each side in seed stitch. Begin the Double Eyelet Rib over the main section of the body. Work 3 repeats of the pattern. Bind off in rib.

SLEEVES

If you're working your sleeve in the round, you'll now need to pick up stitches under the arm to knit the sleeve. Transfer the sleeve stitches to size 8 (5mm) double-pointed or circular needles, (page 13), then pick up and knit 2 stitches under the arm. Join to work in the round.

If you're working the sleeves flat, slip the sleeve stitches to a size 8 needle, work across the row, cast on 2 stitches, work the next row, and cast on 2 stitches. Continue with the pattern, remembering that the first and last stitch are selvedge stitches for the seam and are not part of the lace pattern.

Count your stitches and decrease over the next round to a multiple of 7 plus 2. (Knitters working flat sleeves will need a multiple of 7 plus 4.) Change to smaller needles and work 3 repeats of the Double Eyelet Rib. Bind off in rib.

FINISHING

Sew up sleeves if you worked the sleeves flat. Close any underarm gaps. Weave in all ends.

Make a Custom-Sized Cardi

1. Measure the back of your toy's neck: _____ (N)

2. Note your gauge (stitches per inch/cm): _____ (G)

3. Multiply the back neck measurement by your gauge: (N) x (G) = _____ (N1)

4. Take this result and multiply by 2 to add the sleeve stitches: (N1) x 2 = _____ (N2)

5. The raglan increases surround four "seam" stitches, which help to mark the increase and give a decorative look to the garment. Add these stitches to determine your cast-on number: (N2) + 4 = _____ (CO)

6. Divide N1 by 2 to determine the stitch count for the sleeves: (N1) ÷ 2 = _____ (S)

7. Subtract the seed stitch edging (3 stitches) from the arm stitches to determine your front stitches: (S) – 3 = _____ (F)

Cast on according to your calculations and set up for raglan increases as follows:

Row 1 Knit the seed stitch edge, k(**F**), place marker, k1, place marker, k (**S**), place marker, k1, place marker, k(**N1**), place marker, k1, place marker, k(**S**), place marker, k1, place marker, k(**F**), knit the seed stitch edge.

Follow the main pattern beginning at **Row 2**.

Note: Adjust the sleeve length, sleeve circumference, and body length to fit your bear. If necessary, adjust the number of lace repeats.

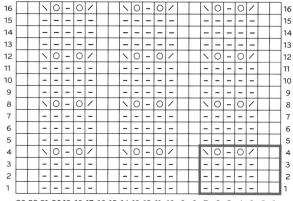

17" [43 cm] total circumference

15" [38 cm] chest circumference

2½" [6.5 cm]

5½" [14 cm]

4" [10 cm]

5" [13 cm]

RIBS AND LACE CHART

	23	22	21	20	19	18	17	16	15	14	13	12	11	10	9	8	7	6	5	4	3	2	1	
16	\	O	–	O	/				\	O	–	O	/				\	O	–	O	/			16
15	–	–	–	–	–				–	–	–	–	–				–	–	–	–	–			15
14	–	–	–	–	–				–	–	–	–	–				–	–	–	–	–			14
13	–	–	–	–	–				–	–	–	–	–				–	–	–	–	–			13
12	\	O	–	O	/				\	O	–	O	/				\	O	–	O	/			12
11	–	–	–	–	–				–	–	–	–	–				–	–	–	–	–			11
10	–	–	–	–	–				–	–	–	–	–				–	–	–	–	–			10
9	–	–	–	–	–				–	–	–	–	–				–	–	–	–	–			9
8	\	O	–	O	/				\	O	–	O	/				\	O	–	O	/			8
7	–	–	–	–	–				–	–	–	–	–				–	–	–	–	–			7
6	–	–	–	–	–				–	–	–	–	–				–	–	–	–	–			6
5	–	–	–	–	–				–	–	–	–	–				–	–	–	–	–			5
4	\	O	–	O	/				\	O	–	O	/				\	O	–	O	/			4
3	–	–	–	–	–				–	–	–	–	–				–	–	–	–	–			3
2	–	–	–	–	–				–	–	–	–	–				–	–	–	–	–			2
1	–	–	–	–	–				–	–	–	–	–				–	–	–	–	–			1

KEY

☐	Knit on RS, purl on WS
–	Purl on RS, knit on WS
\	Ssk
/	K2tog
O	Yarn Over

TRAVELING VINES SUNDRESS

Pearl loves to dress for tea time, and this sundress is one of her favorites. The simple lace inset and contrasting picot hem and edgings make this sleeveless dress perfect for a picnic or garden party.

Skill Level

Intermediate

Finished Measurements

Circumference: 16" (40.5cm)

Length: 10½" (26.5cm), from shoulder to hem

Materials

1 skein Classic Elite Premiere [50% pima cotton, 50% Tencel; 215 yd (197m) per 3½ oz (100g)] color: 5234 cherries jubilee (MC) (3)

1 skein Classic Elite Premiere [50% pima cotton, 50% Tencel; 215 yd (197m) per 3½ oz (100g)] color: 5235 key lime (CC) (3)

Size 7 (4.5mm) circular needles, 24" (61cm) long, or size needed to obtain gauge

Spare size 7 (5mm) circular needle (optional)

Measuring tape

Yarn needle

2 stitch markers

2 stitch holders

Gauge

18 stitches and 25 rows = 4" (10cm) in stockinette stitch

Special Abbreviations

K1-tbl: Knit one stitch through the back loop, twisting the stitch.

P2tog-tbl: Purl two stitches together through the back loop.

Pattern Note

The front is worked back and forth on circular needles, beginning at the bottom hem. You'll work a couple of rows, then make an eyelet row. These first rows are then turned under, forming the picot edging, and secured in place with a three-needle non-bind-off (page 12).

DRESS
FRONT

Using CC and a provisional cast-on over spare needle or waste yarn (page 11), cast on 37 stitches.

Work 2 rows in stockinette stitch, beginning with a knit row.
On the next right-side row, work the picots: K1, *yo, k2tog; repeat from * across.
Work 2 more rows in stockinette stitch.

CREATE HEM

Place the 37 stitches from the provisional cast-on onto a size 8 needle if necessary. Fold the knitting in half with wrong sides facing, and align stitches from the provisional cast-on with the stitches on the working needle. Using CC and the right-hand side of the working needle, work the three-needle non-bind-off (page 12) to knit together stitches from working needle and provisional cast-on, forming the hem. Continue to work the next (purl) row using MC.

Set up for the lace insert

Place markers on either side of the center 13 stitches to mark the location of the lace insert.

LACE INSERT

Note: The lace insert and armhole shaping are worked simultaneously.

Begin to work the lace pattern across the marked center 13 stitches (see stitch chart on page 27), continuing in stockinette stitch on either side.

Note: Right-side rows will end with 1 extra stitch. Wrong-side rows will bring you back to the original stitch count.

Row 1 (RS) Knit to the marker, k2, yo, k1-tbl, yo, ssk, knit to the end of the row.
Row 2 Purl to the marker, p7, p2tog-tbl, purl to the end of the row.
Row 3 Knit to the marker, k2, yo, k1-tbl, yo, k1, ssk, knit to the end of the row.
Row 4 Purl to the marker, p5, p2tog-tbl, purl to the end of the row.
Row 5 Knit to the marker, k2, k1-tbl, yo, k4, ssk, k1, yo, knit to the end of the row.
Row 6 Purl to the marker, p4, p2tog-tbl, purl to the end of the row.
Row 7 Knit to the marker, k7, k2tog, yo, k1-tbl, yo, knit to the end of the row.
Row 8 Purl to the marker, p6, p2tog, purl to the end of the row.
Row 9 Knit to the marker, k5, k2tog, k2, yo, k1-tbl, yo, knit to the end of the row.
Row 10 Purl to the marker, p8, p2tog, purl to the end of the row.
Row 11 Knit to the marker, k2, yo, k1, k2tog, k4, yo, k1-tbl, knit to the end of the row.
Row 12 Purl to the marker, p3, p2tog, purl to the end of the row.
Work **Rows 1–12** three times, then continue to work the lace pattern one more time, while AT THE SAME TIME beginning the armhole shaping.

ARMHOLE SHAPING

Row 1 (RS) K2, ssk, knit to marker; working lace insert between the markers, knit to the last 4 stitches, k2tog, k2.
Row 2 Purl, working the lace insert between the markers.

Repeat **Rows 1 and 2** twice more (6 stitches decreased).

Work the remainder of the lace repeat without further armhole shaping.

RIGHT SHOULDER

Row 1 (RS) K9, remove the next marker, bind off the 13 lace insert stitches, remove the next marker, k9. Slide the stitches from the left shoulder onto a holder and continue to work the right shoulder only.
Row 2 P9.
Row 3 K2, k2tog, k2tog, knit to the end of the row—7 stitches remain.
Row 4 Purl.
Rows 5 and 6 Repeat Rows 3 and 4—5 stitches remain.
Rows 7–10 Work in stockinette stitch.
Do not bind off. Place the 5 Right Shoulder stitches onto a holder.

LEFT SHOULDER

Return the Left Shoulder stitches to the needle, join MC at the neck edge, and begin neck and right shoulder shaping:
Row 1 K9.
Row 2 P9.
Row 3 K2, ssk, ssk, knit to the end of the row—7 stitches remain.
Row 4 Purl.
Rows 5 and 6 Repeat **Rows 3 and 4—5** stitches remain.
Rows 7–10 Work in stockinette stitch.
Do not bind off. Place the 5 Left Shoulder stitches onto a holder.

BACK

Note: The Back is worked the same as the Front, omitting the lace pattern.

Make a Custom-Sized Sundress

1. Measure your toy's lower body circumference at the widest point (on my bear, it's the hips, not the waist): _______ (H)

2. Note your gauge (stitches per inch/cm): _______ (G)

3. Multiply the circumference by your gauge, adding 1 stitch if necessary to make your cast-on an odd number: (H) x (G) = _______ (CO)

Cast on according to your calculations and follow the instructions for the main pattern. Adjust the length of the dress as necessary, remembering you'll need a multiple of 12 rows for a complete lace repeat.

Note: For a very small bear, where the lace insert in the pattern gauge might cover the majority of the bear's chest, consider using a finer gauge yarn.

Using CC and a provisional cast-on (page 11), cast on 37 stitches.

Work 2 rows in stockinette stitch, beginning with a knit row.

On the next right-side row, work the picots: K1, *yo, k2tog; repeat from * across.

Work 2 more rows in stockinette stitch.

CREATE HEM

Place the 37 stitches from the provisional cast-on onto a size 8 needle if necessary. Fold the knitting in half with wrong sides facing, and align stitches from the provisional cast-on with the stitches on the working needle. Using CC, work the three-needle non-bind-off (page 12) and right-hand side of working needle to knit together stitches from working needle and provisional cast-on, forming the hem. Then, continue to work the next (purl) row using MC.

After creating the picot hem, work even in stockinette stitch (no lace) for 36 rows.

RIGHT SHOULDER

Row 1 (RS) K9, remove the next marker, bind off the center 13 stitches, remove the next marker, k9. Slide the stitches from the left shoulder onto a holder and continue to work the right shoulder only.

Row 2 P9.

Row 3 K2, k2tog, k2tog, knit to the end of the row—7 stitches remain.

Row 4 Purl.

Rows 5 and 6 Repeat Rows 3 and 4 (5 stitches remain).

Rows 7–10 Work in stockinette stitch. Do not bind off. Place the 5 Right Shoulder stitches onto a holder.

LEFT SHOULDER

Return the Left Shoulder stitches to the needle, join MC at the neck edge, and begin neck and right shoulder shaping:

Row 1 K9.

Row 2 P9.

Row 3 K2, ssk, ssk, knit to the end of the row (7 stitches remain).

Row 4 Purl.

Rows 5 and 6 Repeat Rows 3 and 4 (5 stitches remain).

Rows 7–10 Work in stockinette stitch. Do not bind off. Place the 5 Left Shoulder stitches onto a holder.

FINISHING

With the Back and Front held with right-sides together, use a three-needle bind-off to join each shoulder.

Sew side seams.

PICOT EDGINGS

Using CC and size 8 needles, pick up stitches evenly around each armhole and the neckline. Work a picot bind-off: *Cast on 2 stitches, bind off 4; repeat from * around.

Weave in all ends.

TRAVELING VINES CHART

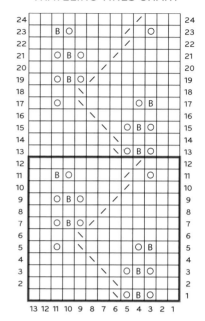

KEY

☐	Knit on rs, purl on ws
B	RS; Knit through back loop. WS: Purl th
\	RS: ssk, WS: p2tog through back loop
/	RS: Kktog, WS: p2tpg
O	Yarn Over

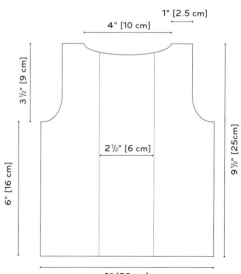

BEAR-T SWEATER

Eddie finds this slouchy ribbed T-shirt perfect for picnic time, as the ribs catch any crumbs he might want to snack on later. Knit in a sideways rib, this classic T-shirt combines sideways knitting with a top-down set-in sleeve.

Skill Level

Beginner

Finished Measurements

T-Shirt Length: 7½" (19cm)

Sleeve Length from Shoulder to Cuff: 5" (12.5cm)

Chest Circumference: 19" (48cm)

Materials

1 skein Galler Yarns Inca Cotton [100% organic cotton; 325 yd (300m) per 8 oz (228g)], color: sage, (5) bulky

Size 9 (5.5mm) needles

Measuring tape

Yarn needle

Gauge

16 stitches and 22 rows = 4" (10cm) in k3, p3 rib

Pattern Note

The sweater is worked in two identical pieces from side to side, casting on at the side seam, and then shaping the first shoulder, the neck, and the second shoulder before binding off at the opposite side seam.

FRONT AND BACK
(Make 2)

FIRST SIDE AND ARMHOLE

Cast on 12 stitches.
Work in k3, p3 rib for 1" (2.5cm), ending with a wrong-side row.

Shape the First Shoulder

On the next right-side row, work in pattern across to the end of the row, cast on 18 stitches.

Continue in pattern for 2" (5cm), ending with a right-side row.

Shape the Neck

On the next wrong-side row, bind off 6 stitches, and then work in pattern to the end of the row.

Continue to work in pattern for 4" (10cm), ending with a wrong-side row.

Shape Second Shoulder

On the next right-side row, work in pattern across all stitches, then cast on 6 stitches at the end of the row. Continue in pattern for 2" (5cm), ending with a right-side row.

SECOND ARMHOLE

Next row (WS) Bind off 18 stitches, work to the end of the row in pattern.
Work in pattern for 1" (2.5cm).

Bind off all stitches in pattern.

SLEEVES
(Make 2)

Note: The sleeves are worked from the shoulder to the cuff.
Cast on 9 stitches.
Row 1 (WS) Work in k3, p3 rib.
Row 2 Kf&b, work in pattern to the last stitch, kf&b.
Continue to increase at the beginning and end of each row, working all of the new stitches into the k3, p3 pattern.

Work the increases until the side (angled) edges measure 3½" (9cm). Work even in pattern for 3" (7.5cm). Bind off all stitches in pattern.

FINISHING

Sew the Front to the Back at the shoulders.

Set in the Sleeve

Center the top of the sleeve cap (the cast-on edge) with the center of the armhole and pin in place. Pin angled edges of sleeves to armhole edges. Pin straight edge of sleeve to side edge of armhole. Sew into place. Repeat for second sleeve.

Sew side and sleeve seams in one line.

Weave in all ends.

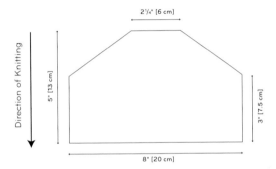

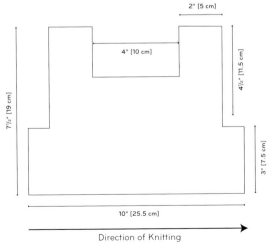

Make a Custom-Sized Bear-T

1. Measure the length of your toy from its underarm to the top of its hips (or where you'd like the T-shirt to fall): _____ (K)

2. Measure from the wrist to the top of the shoulder: _____ (S)

3. Measure the back of your bear's neck: _____ (N)

4. Note your gauge (stitches per inch/cm): _____ (G)

5. Measure your bear's shoulder width _____ (SW)

Multiply your lenght by your gauge to determine you cast-on (CO). Adjust the number to a multiple of 3. (K) × (G) = _____ (CO)

Cast on according to your calculations, and begin by working in the k3, p3 rib pattern for about 1" (2.5cm)—shorter if you have a very skinny bear.

Add the first shoulder

Multiply the shoulder height by your gauge to determine the cast-on for the shoulder (SCO). Adjust the number to a multiple of 3. (S) × (G) = _____ (SCO)

Work in pattern across the width of the bear's shoulder (SW). End on a right-side row.

Shape the Neck

On the next wrong-side row, bind off ⅓ of the shoulder cast-on: (SCO) ÷ 3 = _____ (B), and work in pattern to end.
Continue in pattern for (N)"/cm, ending with a wrong-side row.

Add the Left Shoulder

Cast on left shoulder stitches (B). Continue in pattern for (SW). End on a right-side row.

Left Armhole

On the next wrong-side row, bind off all shoulder cast-on stitches (SCO), work in pattern to the end of the row.
Work in pattern for 1" (2.5cm), or to match the right side.

Bind off all stitches in pattern.

Sleeves (Make 2)

Cast on half the shoulder cast-on stitches: (SCO) ÷ 2 (rounding to make it a multiple of 3 if necessary) = _____ .
Follow the main pattern, increasing until the measurements of the side edges plus the measurement of the cast-on edge is equal to (S) x 2. You can verify this by positioning the sleeve in the armhole.

Work even in pattern for 2" (5cm) or longer if you'd like a longer sleeve.

Bind off all stitches in pattern. Assemble the T-shirt according to the main pattern instructions.

A Teddy Bear's Picnic

LETTER SWEATER

Joey's basic play "uniform" includes his blue jeans and this Letter Sweater. The comfy sweater is knit in a soft, marled organic cotton-wool blend and uses a basic drop shoulder construction. Add a letter "B" formed with an easy knit and purl pattern for a collegiate touch.

Skill Level

Easy

Finished Measurements

Chest Circumference: 16" (40.5cm)

Back Length: 5¾" (14.5cm) from neck to hem

Sleeve Length: 4" (10cm)

Sleeve Width: 6" (15cm)

Materials

2 skeins Vermont Organics O-Wool Balance [50% certified organic merino, 50% certified organic cotton; 130 yd (120m) per 1¾ oz (50g)] color: amber, (4) medium

Size 7 (4.5mm) knitting needles

Measuring tape

Yarn needle

3 stitch holders

Gauge

18 stitches and 28 rows = 4" (10cm) in stockinette stitch.

Starting with a wrong-side row, work in stockinette stitch for 13 rows.

Work the Letter Chart (page 34)

On the next right-side row, begin the charted letter design: K13, place marker, work across 14-stitch chart, place marker, k13. Continue working the chart between the markers and working stockinette stitch outside the markers.

After completing the 16 rows of the chart, work 5 more rows in stockinette stitch.

Shape the Neck and the Right Shoulder

Row 1 (RS) K28, ssk, k10.
Row 2 (WS) P9, p2tog, and place these 10 stitches on a holder for the right shoulder; place the next 16 stitches on a holder for the front neck.

Shape the Left Shoulder

Row 1 Rejoin yarn at the neck edge of the left shoulder, p2tog, p10.
Row 2 K9, K2tog. Place these 10 stitches on a holder.

SLEEVES

(Make 2)

The sleeves are worked from the shoulder to the cuff.
Cast on 32 stitches. Starting with a purl row, work in stockinette stitch for 3½" (9cm).
Switch to k1, p1 ribbing and work 3 rows. Bind off in rib pattern.

Pattern Notes

If you want to change the "B" chart to another letter you can easily find letter charts on the Internet or even draw your own on graph paper—draw the outline of a letter lightly onto the graph paper, then fill in the squares to mark where the purl stitches will go.

For a more colorful sweater, you could work the "B" chart in intarsia (colorwork) instead of purl stitches. Or, work the body in plain stockinette stitch and work the chart in a 2nd color after the fact using duplicate stitch or embroidery.

BACK

Cast on 40 stitches.

Work 3 rows in k1, p1 rib. The piece should measure about ½" (13mm).
Starting with a wrong-side row, work in stockinette stitch until the piece measures 6" (15cm) from the cast-on edge. End with a wrong-side row.

Divide the stitches onto three stitch holders: 10 stitches for right shoulder, 20 stitches for the back neck, and 10 stitches for the left shoulder. Cut the yarn, leaving a 6" (15cm) tail and set the Back aside.

FRONT

Cast on 40 stitches.
Work 3 rows in k1, p1 rib. The piece should measure about ½" (13mm).

FINISHING

Join the shoulder seams using a three-needle bind-off.

NECK EDGING

Starting from the right shoulder seam, pick up and knit 4 stitches to the front neckline holder, knit the 16 stitches on the holder, pick up and knit 4 stitches to the left shoulder seam, knit the 20 stitches on the holder for the back neck—44 stitches.

Work 3 rows of k1, p1 rib.
Bind off in ribbing.

Block all four pieces. Weave in all ends. Match the center of the cast-on edge of the sleeve to the shoulder seam. Sew the Sleeves to the sides of the sweater. Sew up the sleeve and side seams.

Make a Custom-Sized Letter Sweater

1. Measure the width of your toy's chest at the widest point, and add 1" (2.5cm) for ease: _____ (C)

2. Note your gauge (stitches per inch/cm): _____ (G)

3. Multiply your chest measurement by your gauge, adding 1 stitch if necessary to make your cast-on an even number: (C) x (G)= _____ (CO)

4. Measure your bear's arm circumference at its widest point and add 1" (2.5cm) for ease: _____ (A)

5. Multiply the adjusted arm measurement by your gauge to determine your sleeve cast-on: (A) x (G) = _____ (SCO).

Cast on according to your calculations and work the instructions as written with the following changes:

Divide the cast-on number by 4 to calculate the number of stitches for each shoulder. (Use this number when working the decreases for the front neck opening).

Divide the cast-on number by 2 to calculate the number of stitches for the neck. Put this number of stitches on the holder for the back neck; the front neck will have 4 fewer stitches because of the neck decreases.

Note: The "B" chart is worked over 14 stitches centered on the front of the sweater. If you're working the sweater for a very small bear, consider using a finer gauge yarn so the letter does not take up too much of the bear's chest.

For the sleeves, cast on according to your calculations, and knit the sleeves as specified in the pattern, adjusting the length as necessary for your bear.

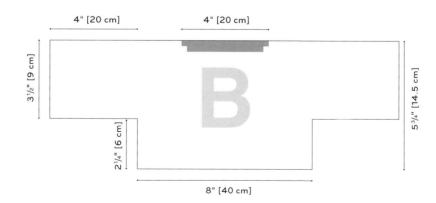

LETTER SWEATER STITCH CHART

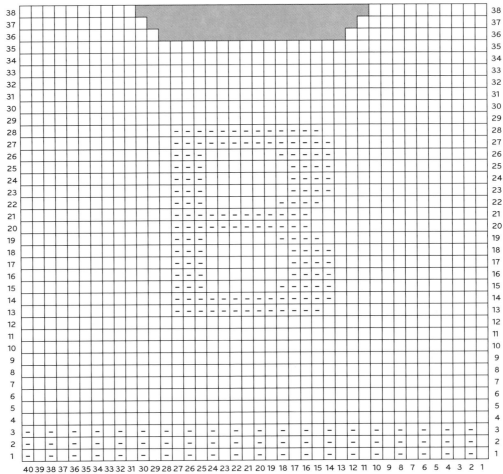

KEY

☐ Knit on RS, purl on WS

– Purl on RS, knit on WS

BERRY BOLERO

Skill Level

Beginner

Finished Measurements

Chest Circumference: 15" (38cm)

Length: 4½" (11.5cm)

Sleeve: 3½" (9cm) from neck to cuff

Materials

1 skein Knit One, Crochet Too Ty-Dy [100% cotton; 196 yd (180m) per 3½ oz (100g)], color: 672, (4) medium

Size 7 (4.5mm) circular needles, 24" (61cm) long, or size needed to obtain gauge

Measuring tape

Yarn needle

Stitch markers

Stitch holders

Gauge

20 stitches x 30 rows = 4" (10cm) in stockinette stitch

Besides honey, berries are one of Pearl's favorite treats. Luckily, this tie-dyed cotton yarn is the perfect thing to hide a stain from the odd berry that slips out of her paw. Knit in one piece from the neck down, this bolero is nearly finished when you bind off at the waist. Just add a bit of garter stitch edging around the openings and sleeves, and it's ready to wear.

Special Stitches

L-Rinc (Lifted Right Increase): Lift the right leg of the stitch below the stitch on the left needle, knit into that leg, then knit the stitch on the needle.

L-Linc (Lifted Left Increase): Knit the next stitch on the left needle, then insert the left needle into the left leg of the stitch two rows below the stitch on the right needle, and knit into that leg.

BOLERO

Cast on 48 stitches.

Set up for the raglan increases and begin the neck shaping

Row 1 (WS) Kf&b, k1, place marker, k1, place marker, k10, place marker, k1, place marker, k20, place marker, k1, place marker, k10, place marker, k1, place marker, k1, kf&b.

Row 2 Purl.

Begin raglan increases and continue the neck shaping

Row 1 Kf&b, *knit to the first marker, L-rinc, slip marker (slip marker), k1, slip marker, L-linc; repeat from * 4 times, knit to the last 2 stitches, k1, kf&b.

Row 2 Purl.

  *A Teddy Bear's Picnic*

Repeat the last 2 rows 4 more times—100 stitches.

The neck shaping is complete. Continue the raglan increases as follows:

Row 1 *Knit to marker, L-rinc, slip marker, k1, slip marker, L-linc; repeat from * 4 times, knit to the end of the row.
Row 2 Purl.

Repeat these 2 rows twice more—124 stitches.

Place the sleeve stitches on holders
Remove the markers as you encounter them in this row. Knit to the 1st marker, place the stitches between the 1st and 4th markers on a holder for the left sleeve; cast on 2 stitches for the underarm, knit across the back to the 5th marker, then place the stitches between the 5th and 8th markers onto a second holder for the right sleeve, cast on 2 stitches for the underarm, knit to the end of the row.

Shape the Bolero
Row 1 (WS) Purl.
Row 2 K1, ssk, knit to the last 3 stitches, k2tog, k1.

Repeat **Rows 1–2** twice more. Work Row 1 once more.

GARTER EDGING
Leaving the stitches on the needle, turn the work, and with the right side facing you, pick up stitches along the side edge of the bolero opening (picking up approximately 3 stitches for every 4 rows), pick up stitches evenly across the back of the neck, and down the opposite side edge. Join to work in the round.
Round 1 Knit.
Round 2 Purl.
Work **Rounds 1 and 2** once more. Repeat **Row 1** once more.
Bind off.

GARTER SLEEVE EDGING
Slide the sleeve stitches from one holder onto the working needles.
Pick up 2 stitches in the gap under the arm.

Join to work in the round. Work as for the Garter Edging. Repeat for the second sleeve.

FINISHING
Weave in all ends.

Make a Custom-Sized Bolero

To make a custom sized Berry Bolero, follow the calculation sidebar on page 18 (from Deep V). Add 1 stitch to each front. Cast on according to your calculations, and begin working the Berry Bolero pattern starting with **Row 2**.

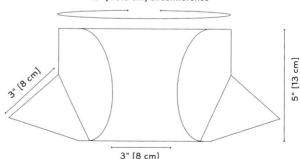

16" [40.5 cm] circumference

3" [8 cm]

3" [8 cm]

5" [13 cm]

BLUE JEANS

Perfect for a Teddy Bear's Picnic or just a walk around the block, these jeans are soft yet rugged. They are knit in one piece starting at the waist, so creating the perfect pair for your favorite bear is a snap!

Skill Level

Adventurous Beginner

Finished Measurements

Waist Circumference: 15" (38cm)

Inseam: 3½" (9cm)

Materials

1 skein Brown Sheep Cotton Fleece [80% cotton, 20% merino wool; 215 yd (197m) per 3½ oz (100g)], color: CW790, Columbine Blossom, (4) medium

Size 7 (4.5 mm) circular needles, 24" (61cm) long, or size needed to obtain gauge

Spare size 7 circular needle (optional)

Size 7 double-pointed needles (optional)

Fabric Pencil

1 skein embroidery floss (for top stitching)

Tapestry needle

Measuring tape

Yarn needle

1 stitch marker

2 stitch holders

Gauge

20 stitches and 30 rows = 4" (10 cm) in stockinette

Using a provisional cast-on over a spare needle or waste yarn (page 11), cast on 68 stitches.

Work 10 rows in stockinette stitch.

WAISTBAND

Fold the knit fabric in half with the wrong sides facing; align the stitches from the provisional cast-on (sliding them onto a needle if they were on waste yarn), with the stitches on the working needle. Work a three-needle non-bind-off to close the casing (page 12). Place a marker to indicate the center front of the jeans and join to work in the round.

Work even in stockinette stitch for 3½" (9 cm).

Setup to work the inseam

Count your stitches and place a removable marker or safety pin directly across from the beginning of round marker, dividing the stitches in half evenly.

Starting at the center front marker, k5,

place marker, knit to 5 stitches before 2nd marker, place marker, k5, remove center back marker, k5, place marker, knit to 5 stitches before beginning of round marker, place marker, k5, remove beginning of round marker. There are 10 stitches marked at the center front and the center back.

INSEAM

The inseam is worked with short rows across the center front 10 stitches to form a flap.
Row 1 (RS) Beginning at marker, k5, turn.
Row 2 (WS) S1 purlwise, p9, turn.
Row 3 S1 knitwise, k9, turn.

Repeat **Rows 2–3** until the inseam flap measures 2½" (6.5cm)

Join the flap to the backside of the jeans

With the right sides together, join the 10 stitches of the inseam together with the 10 stitches opposite them at the center back using a three-needle bind-off (page 12). Fasten off. There will be 24 stitches for each leg on either side of the inseam.

LEGS

Place the stitches for the left leg on a stitch holder.

With right side facing, pick up 12 stitches along the side of the inseam flap on the right leg, pick up 2 stitches at the corner, and join to work in the round. (You can transfer the stitches to double-pointed needles or work in the round on circulars, page 13.)

Work the leg in stockinette stitch for 4" (10cm). Change to reverse stockinette stitch. Work 5 rows. Bind off loosely.

Slide the stitches for the left leg onto the needle. Work as for the right leg.

FINISHING

Finish waistband or create (optional) drawstring. For a smooth waistband, sew closed the opening where you created the hem. This becomes the back of the jeans. For a drawstring closure, crochet a 25" (63.5cm) chain and thread throught the openings created by the hem. The side with the opening becomes the front of the jeans.

Weave in ends.

EMBROIDERY

Using a fabric pencil, lightly draw lines on the jeans to mark the pockets, fly, and waistband. With orange embroidery floss and a needle, use running stitches to create the "jeans" look. Refer to the detail photograph above as a guide.

Make a Custom-Sized Pair of Blue Jeans

1. Measure your toy's lower body at the widest point. (On my bear, it's the hips, not the waist.): _____ (H)

2. Enter your stitch gauge: _____ (G)

3. To calculate the number of stitches to cast on, multiply (G) x (H) = _____ (CO)

Cast on according to your calculations and follow the instructions as written, making sure to measure and adjust the distance from the waist to the inseam and the length of the leg.

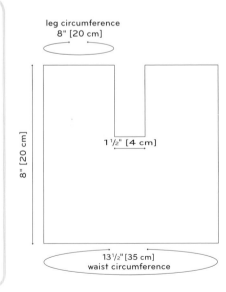

leg circumference
8" [20 cm]

8" [20 cm]

1 1/2" [4 cm]

13 1/2" [35 cm]
waist circumference

Dress-Up

No bear wardrobe would be complete without costumes. Here you'll find Bears in the Kitchen (page 59): a chef's outfit complete with pleated toque and apron. Our drama queen, Pearl, dresses to the nines in her Paparazzi Evening Gown (page 56) and gets ready to hit the stage in her Rock Star Twinset (page 42). Joey models workout gear for a Basketball Star (page 52), and Pearl shows off flippers and a halter top that can turn your favorite bear into a furry little Mermaid (page 49).

ROCK STAR TWINSET

Even Pearl has her rockin' side, and she likes to show it off in this lacy silk shrug and camisole complete with glass bead "bling." Both pieces are simple rectangles. The shrug features a delicate eyelet lace pattern, and both pieces have picot edgings worked in beaded yarn.

Special Stitches

Simple Eyelet Lace (multiple of 6 stitches, plus 2)
Row 1 (RS) Knit.
Row 2 (WS) Purl.
Row 3 K1, *k3, yo, ssk, k1, repeat from * to last stitch, k1.
Row 4 Purl.
Row 5 Knit.
Row 6 Purl.
Row 7 K1, *yo, ssk, k4, repeat from * to last stitch, k1.
Row 8 Purl.
Repeat **Rows 1–8** for pattern.

PICOT BIND-OFF

On a right-side row *cast on 2 stitches, bind off 4 stitches, slip the remaining stitch on the right-hand needle back to the left-hand needle. Repeat from * until 1 stitch remains. Fasten off.

CAMISOLE

Using MC and a provisional cast-on (page 11), cast on 66 stitches.

Work in stockinette stitch for 2" (5cm).

Switch to CC and work the Picot Bind-Off on next right-side row.
Transfer the stitches from the provisionally cast-on edge onto the working needle. With the right side facing and using CC, work the Picot Bind-Off.

I-CORD STRAPS

(make 2)
Using double-pointed needles and CC, cast on 4 stitches.
Work I-cord (page 11) for 8" (20cm).
Secure the ends.

Skill Level

Adventurous Beginner

Finished Measurements

Camisole Chest Circumference: 14.5" (37cm)

Camisole Length (including picots): 3" (7.5cm)

Shrug Width (cuff to cuff, including edging): 13½" (34.5cm)

Materials

1 skein Tilli Tomas Pure and Simple [100% silk; 150 yd (137m) per 3½ oz (100g)], color: arts and crafts (MC), (4) medium

1 skein Tilli Tomas Rock Star [100% silk with glass beads; 100 yd (91m) per 3½ oz (100g)], color: arts and crafts (CC), (4) medium

Size 7 (4.5mm) circular needles, 24" (60cm) long, or size needed to obtain gauge

Size 7 (4.5mm) double-pointed needles (optional, for I-cord)

Measuring tape

Yarn needle

Gauge

18 stitches and 26 rows = 4" (10 cm)

FINISHING

With right sides together, sew the two short sides together. The seam should center in the back of the bear when worn.

Try the camisole on the bear and use safety pins or removable stitch markers to mark where you'd like the straps to go. Sew the straps into place at the markings.

Weave in all ends.

SHRUG

Using MC and a provisional cast-on (page 11), cast on 32 stitches.
Work the Simple Eyelet Pattern for 13" (33cm).

Switch to CC and work the Picot Bind-Off on the next right-side row.
Transfer the stitches from the provisional cast-on to the working needles.
With the right side facing and using CC, work a Picot Bind-Off.

FINISHING

Weave in all ends.

Fold the shrug in half lengthwise. Sew a seam 2" (3cm) long beginning at the picot edge and working toward the center to form a sleeve. Repeat for the opposite side.

SIMPLE EYELET STITCH PATTERN

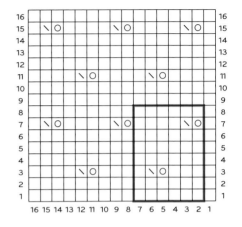

KEY

☐	Knit on RS, purl on WS
╲	Ssk
O	Yarn Over

Make a Custom-Sized Camisole

1. Make a note of your Gauge: _____ (G)

2. Measure the toy's chest circumference: _____ (C)

3. Multiply the circumference by your gauge: (C) x (G) = _____ (CO)

Cast on the number specified above and follow the main pattern as written.

Make a Custom-Sized Shrug

1. Measure your bear's arm circumference: _____ (A)

2. Multiply the circumference by your gauge: (A) x (G) = _____ (S)

3. Adjust (S) to be a multiple of 6 plus 2 to accommodate the lace pattern (adding stitches is preferable to subtracting, since a more generous sleeve works just fine for this project): _____ (CO).

MERLIN'S TAIL WIZARD OUTFIT

When Joey wants to mix potions or stir up a little magic, he dons his wizard's cap and gown. The cap and gown are sprinkled with green intarsia stars. The gown is finished with a picot hem, and is constructed in a simple drop shoulder design. The hat is worked in one piece with minimal finishing.

Skill Level

Intermediate

Finished Measurements

Gown Chest Circumference: 16" (40.5cm)

Gown Length: 11" (28cm)

Gown Sleeve Length: 4" (10cm)

Hat Circumference: 13" (19cm)

Hat Height: 5" (12.5cm)

Materials

2 skeins Vermont Organic Fibers O-Wool [100% organic merino wool; 198 yd (181m) per 3½ oz (100g)], color: black (MC), medium

1 skein Vermont Organic Fibers O-Wool [100% organic merino wool; 198 yd (181m) per 3½ oz (100g)], color: green (CC), medium

Size 7 (4.5mm) needles, or size needed to obtain gauge

Spare size 7 (4.5mm) circular needle, any length, for provisional cast-on

Size 7 (4.5mm) double-pointed needles for I-cord edging

stitch markers

2 buttons, ½" (13mm) diameter each

Gauge

20 stitches and 32 rows = 4" (10cm) in stockinette stitch

WIZARD'S GOWN

BACK

The body is worked back and forth on circular needles beginning at the bottom hem. You'll work a couple of rows, and then make an eyelet row. These first rows are then turned under, forming the picot edging, and secured in place with a three-needle non-bind-off (page 12).

Using MC and a provisional cast-on over spare needle or waste yarn (page 11), cast on 50 stitches.

Work 2 rows in stockinette stitch, beginning with a knit row.
Next row (RS) *k2tog, yo, repeat from * to the last 2 stitches, k2.
Work 2 more rows in stockinette stitch.

CREATE HEM

Fold the knitting in half with the wrong sides facing and align the stitches from the provisional cast-on with the stitches on the working needle. Using CC, work the three needle non-bind-off (page 12) to knit together stitches from the working needle and the provisional cast-on, forming the picot hem—50 stitches.

Next row (WS) Purl with MC.
Note: Read through the following instructions before proceeding. You will be working the intarsia chart as you continue decreasing.

Begin gown decreases

On the next right-side row begin to decrease: K1, ssk, knit to last 3 stitches, k2tog, k1.
Repeat the decrease row every 6th row.

STAR CHART

Join CC and begin Intarsia Chart (page 48), on Row 8, and, **at the same time**, continue decreasing every 6th row as set. Work decreases a total of 5 times—40 stitches.

After finishing the intarsia chart, continue in stockinette stitch with MC only until the piece measures 10" (25.5 cm), ending with a wrong-side row.

SHOULDERS AND BUTTONHOLES

Row 1 K10; slide the next 20 stitches on a holder for the neck, k10. (left shoulder)
Row 2 P10, slide right shoulder stitches onto a holder.
Row 3 (buttonhole row) K2, k2tog, yo, k2, k2tog, yo, k2.
Row 4 Purl.
Bind off left shoulder.

FRONT

Work as for the Back until the piece measures 9½" (24 cm), ending with a wrong-side row.

Shoulders, and Neck Shaping

Row 1 (RS) K28, ssk, k10.
Row 2 P9, p2tog—10 stitches.
Break yarn and place these 10 stitches on a holder for the right shoulder; place next 16 stitches on holder for front neck; rejoin yarn for left shoulder, p2tog, p10.
Row 3 K9, k2tog.
Row 4 Purl.
Bind off right shoulder.

FINISHING

Join the right shoulder using a three-needle bind-off (page 12).

NECKBAND

With CC and starting at the left front shoulder, pick up and knit 3 stitches on the side of the neck, knit the 16 stitches from the front neck holder, pick up and knit 3 stitches on the side of the neck to the shoulder seam, knit the 20 stitches from the back neck holder, pick up and knit 3 stitches on the side of the neck on the buttonhole band—45 stitches.

ATTACHED I-CORD EDGING

Using a double-pointed needle, cast on 3 stitches and knit 1 row. WITHOUT turning the needle, * slip the three stitches back to right end of the needle; pulling yarn tightly from end of row, knit 2 stitches, and then knit the 3rd stitch together with the FIRST stitch from the neck edge. WITHOUT turning the needle, slip the 3 stitches back to the right end; pulling yarn tightly from end of row, repeat from * until you have worked all the stitches from the neck edge. Bind off the remaining stitches.

SLEEVES

(make two)
Sleeves are worked from the top down.

INTARSIA CHART (CAP)

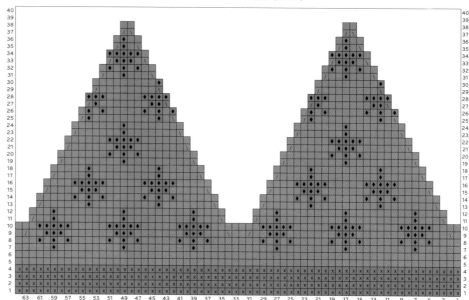

With MC, cast on 32 stitches.

Row 1 (WS) Purl.

Row 2 Knit.

Row 3 Purl.

Row 4 K1fb, knit to last 2 stitches, k1fb, k1.

Repeat these 4 rows 5 times more—44 stitches.

Work even until the sleeve measures 4" (10cm), ending with a wrong-side row.

KEY

I	Knit both sides	/	SSK: Slip, Slip Knit
⊕	Yarn Over	/.	Purl 2 together
\	Knit 2 together	♦	Green
.\	Purl 2 together thru back		

Make a Custom-Sized Wizard's Cap

1. Measure your toy's head circumference: _____ (C)

2. Make a note of your gauge: _____ (G)

3. Multiply your gauge by the head measurement: G x C = _____ (S)

4. Adjust (S) by rounding up to a multiple of 4: _____ (CO)

Cast on according to your calculations and work the hat according to the instructions. You may need to adjust the placement of the intarsia stars. When you set up for the decreases, divide your stitches by 4 and place your markers accordingly.

Make a Custom-Sized Wizard's Gown

The wizard's gown uses simple shapes that can easily be resized, but you may want to adjust the placement of the stars. You can work the stars at any point on the front or back. If you're making a small gown, you could use the stars from the hat on the gown as well.

1. Begin by measuring across your toy's chest from underarm to underarm: _____ (C)

2. Make a note of your gauge: _____ (G)

3. Increase the chest measurement by 130% to get the width of the gown at the hem: (C) x 1.3 = _____ (H)

4. Multiply your gauge by the hem width to get your cast-on number: (G) x (H) = _____ (CO)

Work the instructions as written (adjusting star placement as necessary). When decreasing the edges of the gown, decrease until the front or back is approximately the width of the

bear's chest plus 1" (2.5cm) of ease. Count the number of stitches on the needle at the chest and divide by 4 to calculate the number of stitches for each shoulder. Adjust the length of the gown as necessary.

To work the sleeves, measure the circumference of your bear's arm and add ½" (1.3cm) of ease. Multiply your measurement by your gauge to get your cast-on number for the sleeves. Work as directed in the instructions, adjusting the length as necessary.

INTARSIA CHART (GOWN)

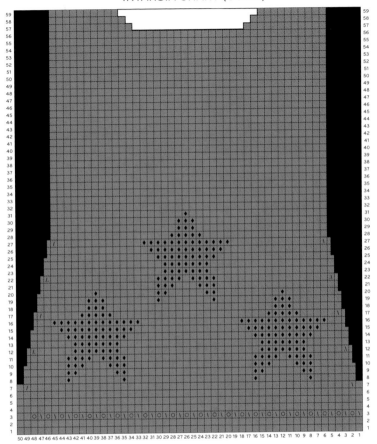

PICOT HEM

Next row (RS) *K2tog, yo, repeat from * to the last 2 stitches, k2.
Work 2 more rows in stockinette stitch.
Bind off.

Fold the hem to the inside of the sleeve and sew in place.

ASSEMBLY

Overlap the shoulder edges of the buttonhole and the button bands, and baste the edges together to make it easier to sew the sleeve into place. Place the middle of the upper edge of the sleeves in line with the shoulder seams, and sew the sleeves to the gown. Sew sleeve and side seams.

Remove the basting stitches. Weave in all ends. Block to measurements.

WIZARD'S CAP

The cap is worked flat and then sewn in the back.

With CC, cast on 64 stitches. Knit 5 rows in garter stitch.

Change to MC and work 2 rows in stockinette stitch, placing markers every 16 stitches (4 markers placed).

Begin decreases and intarsia chart

Begin the Intarsia Chart (page 47), and on next right-side row, begin the cap decreases:
Row 1 (RS) *Knit to 2 stitches before the marker, k2tog; repeat from * across—60 stitches remaining.
Row 2 Purl.
Repeat these 2 rows 14 times while following the Intarsia Chart (4 stitches remain after the decreases are complete).
Cut the yarn leaving a 10" (25.5cm) tail. Thread the yarn onto a tapestry needle and draw through the 4 remaining stitches. Pull the yarn to tighten, put the yarn to the wrong side, and secure the end.

FINISHING

Weave in all ends. Sew the seam up the back of the cap.

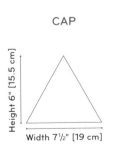

CAP

Height 6" [15.5 cm]
Width 7½" [19 cm]

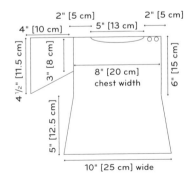

2" [5 cm]
2" [5 cm]
4" [10 cm]
5" [13 cm]
4½" [11.5 cm]
3" [8 cm]
8" [20 cm] chest width
6" [15 cm]
5" [12.5 cm]
10" [25 cm] wide

MERMAID

Is she a bear or is she a mermaid? When Pearl plays dress-up she really gets into her role, and wearing this mermaid costume is no exception. The flipper skirt and cute halter top are worked in shiny and luxurious bamboo yarn that looks as if it just slipped out of the sea.

Skill Level

Beginner

Finished Measurements

Halter Length: 3" (7.5cm)

Width: 6½" (16.5cm) not including ties

Flipper Length: 7½" (19cm)

Flipper Circumference at Waist: 15" (38cm)

Materials

1 skein of Alchemy Yarns of Transformation Bamboo [100% bamboo; 138 yd (126m) per 1¾ oz (50g)], color: slip stream (MC), (3) light

1 skein of Alchemy Yarns of Transformation Bamboo [100% bamboo; 138 yd (126m) per 1¾ oz (50g)], color: teal tide (CC), (3) light

Size 7 (4.5mm) needles, or size needed to obtain gauge

Size 5 (3.5mm) needles

Size 7 (4.5mm) crochet hook

Measuring tape

Optional: a small amount of synthetic fiber stuffing or roving to fill out the flippers

Yarn needle

Gauge

26 stitches and 28 rows = 4" (10 cm)

HALTER

Using MC, cast on 18 stitches.

Rows 1 and 2 Knit.

Row 3 (RS) K2, (m1, k1) 3 times, knit to last 5 stitches, (k1, m1) 3 times, k2—24 stitches.

Row 4 (WS) Purl.

Repeat **Rows 3 and 4** three more times— 42 stitches.

Cast on for the ties

Row 1 (RS) Before beginning to knit the next row, cast on 36 stitches. Knit to the end of the row, cast on 36 stitches—114 stitches.

Row 2 Purl.

Work in stockinette stitch for 6 rows.

Bind off.

FINISHING

Beginning at the end of one tie, join CC and, using a size 7 (4.5mm) crochet hook, single crochet evenly around all edges of the halter. (page 13) Fasten off.

Weave in ends.

Optional: Use a short piece of yarn to cinch the center front of the halter as shown in the photograph.

Make a Custom-Sized Halter

1. Measure the toy's chest between its shoulders: _____ (S)

2. Make a note of your gauge: _____ (G)

3. Multiply your measurement by your gauge to get your cast-on: (G) x (S) = _____ (CO)

Cast on according to your calculations and follow the pattern as written, adjusting the length of the halter to suit your bear. You can also add or remove stitches cast on for the ties to make them shorter or longer.

FLIPPERS

Using size 5 (3.5mm) needles and MC, cast on 48 stitches.

Rows 1–3 Work in k1, p1 rib.

Row 4 (RS) Switch to size 7 (4.5mm) needles and knit all stitches.

Row 5 Purl.

Row 6 (Eyelet drawstring row) K2, *k4, yarn over; repeat from * to last 2 stitches, k2—59 stitches.

Work even in stockinette stitch until the piece measures 3" (7.5cm) from the cast-on edge, ending with a wrong-side row.

FLIPPER DECREASES

Row 1 (RS) K1, ssk, knit to the last 3 stitches, k2tog, k1.

Rows 2–4 Work even in stockinette stitch.

Repeat **Rows 1–4** until 41 stitches remain.

The piece will measure about 6" (15cm) across. End with a wrong-side row.

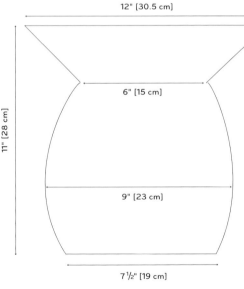

12" [30.5 cm]

6" [15 cm]

11" [28 cm]

9" [23 cm]

7¹⁄₂" [19 cm]

FLIPPER INCREASES

Row 1 (RS) k1, m1, k1, m1, knit to the last two stitches, m1, k1, m1, k1.
Row 2 Purl.

Repeat **Rows 1 and 2** until you have 76 stitches. The flipper will measure about 12" (30.5cm) across.
Place the stitches from the front onto a holder.
Repeat instructions in CC for the Back.

FINISHING

Slide the stitches from the front onto a needle, hold both pieces of fabric with right sides together and work a three-needle bind-off to join the bottom edge of the flipper.
Sew side seams.
Weave in all ends.

Crochet a chain 24" (61cm) long and thread through eyelet holes for the drawstring.

Optional: Using a 6" (15cm) piece of yarn, thread the yarn through a center front stitch about 2" (5cm) up from the bottom edge. Tie the yarn to cinch the center of the flipper. Stuff the flipper with a little wool or synthetic fiber filling.

BASKETBALL STAR

A team player, Joey loves sporting his school colors in his basketball shorts, tank, and sweatband. Knit in an unusual polypropylene and soy "wicking" yarn, this outfit keeps Joey cool on the court or anywhere he is going to be active. The drawstring shorts are knit in two identical pieces and finished with simple side seams. The tank is knit in one piece from the neck down, making it a cinch to get a custom fit.

Pattern Note

The Basketball Tank is worked seamlessly from the top. After a provisional cast-on, the straps are created first and the front pieces are transferred to holders while the back is worked. Once the armholes are shaped for front and back, the pieces are joined and the remainder of the body is worked in the round. This construction allows for easy customization, because you can try the tank on your bear as you go to get a perfect fit.

TANK
FRONT
RIGHT SHOULDER

With MC, using a provisional cast-on (page 11), cast on 10 stitches.
Row 1 Knit.
Row 2 K2, purl to the last 2 stitches, k2.

Repeat **Rows 1 and 2** until the piece measures 2" (5cm), ending with a wrong-side row.
Leave this piece on the needles.

LEFT SHOULDER

Turn the work so the right side is facing. With a second ball of yarn, provisionally cast on 10 stitches. Work as for the right shoulder. Break off the yarn, but do not bind off.

Join the shoulder pieces

Row 1 Pick up the yarn from the Right Shoulder. Knit across these 10 stitches, cable cast on 15 stitches, knit across the 10 stitches of the Left Shoulder. There are 35 stitches on the needle.
Row 2 K2, purl to last 2 stitches, k2.

Skill Level

Adventurous Beginner

Finished Measurements

Shorts: 9" (23cm) wide, 5½" (14 cm) long

Tank: 9" (23cm) wide, 4½" (11.5cm) long

Armhole depth: 2½" (6.5cm)

Neck opening: 3" (7.5cm)

U-neck depth: 2" (5cm)

Materials

2 skeins Knit One Crochet Too Wick [53% soy, 47% polypropylene; 120 yd (109m) per 1¾ oz (50g)], color: 688 cornflower (MC), **(4)** medium

1 skein Knit One Crochet Too Wick [53% soy, 47% Polypropylene; 120 yd (109m) per 1¾ oz (50g)], color: 464 gold (CC), **(4)** medium

Size 7 (4.5mm) circular knitting needles, or size needed to obtain gauge

Size 7 (4.5mm) crochet hook

1¼" (3cm) number appliqué

Measuring tape

Yarn needle

Gauge

20 stitches and 30 rows per 4" (10cm) in stockinette

Begin the armhole shaping

Row 1 K3, kf&b, knit to last 5 stitches, kf&b, k4—2 stitches increased.
Row 2 K2, purl to last 2 stitches, k2.

Repeat **Rows 1 and 2** 4 times more (10 stitches added). Break yarn, but do not bind off.
Slip Front stitches onto a stitch holder.

BACK

Row 1 With the right side facing, place the 10 stitches from the provisional cast-on for the Left Shoulder onto the working needle. Knit across, cast on 15 stitches, transfer the 10 stitches for the Right Shoulder to the left needle; knit across—35 stitches.
Row 2 (WS) K2, purl to last 2 stitches, k2.

Continue to work in pattern as set for 2" (5cm), and then work the armhole shaping as for Front. End with a wrong-side row.

JOIN THE FRONT AND BACK

On the next right-side row, knit across the Back, then transfer stitches for the Front from the holder to the left-hand needle; knit across the Front stitches with the same strand of yarn, joining the pieces to work in the round. Knit a total of two rounds with MC.

Change to CC. Knit 3 rounds.

Change to MC. Work in k1, p1 rib for 4 rounds.
Bind off.

Make a Custom-Sized Tank

1. Measure the toy's shoulder from neck to shoulder edge: _____ (S)

2. Record your gauge: _____ (G)

3. Multiply (G) x (S) = _____ (CO)

Cast on according to your calculations above, and follow instructions for the main pattern, keeping in mind the following notes:

For each shoulder strap, knit half the length from the toy's neck to the toy's waist, and then cast on for the neck opening. Work the Back the same way.

The stitches cast on for the neck opening should be 1½ times the number of stitches on one shoulder, on both the Front and the Back.

The number of stitches added to the Front and the Back for the armhole shaping should be approximately the same as the stitches cast on for the first shoulder (That is, if you cast on 10 for the left shoulder, you'll increase 10 stitches total, or 1 stitch at each edge every right-side row, five times. But you can also hold the top up to the bear as you go to see when you've increased enough.)

Use the toy as your guide when determining the length of the tank. You can make it as long as desired.

FINISHING

Optional: Using size 7 (4.5mm) crochet hook, single crochet evenly around the neck opening (page 13).

Weave in all ends.

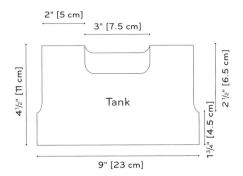

2" [5 cm]
3" [7.5 cm]
4½" [11 cm]
2½" [6.5 cm]
1¾" [4.5 cm]
Tank
9" [23 cm]

SHORTS
BACK AND FRONT

(make 2)
Using MC, cast on 44 stitches.
Work 4 rows of k1, p1 ribbing, ending with a wrong-side row.

Drawstring Panel

Row 1 (RS) Knit.
Row 2 Purl.
Row 3 *K4, yo; repeat from * to last the 4 stitches, k4—53 stitches.

Work even in stockinette stitch for 2" (5cm), ending with a wrong-side row.

Divide for Legs

Use 2 balls of yarn to work both legs at once as follows:

Row 1 K27, join a second ball of yarn, knit to the end with second ball of yarn.

Row 2 Purl across the first leg, switch to the second ball at the leg opening, purl to the end of the row.

Continue to work on both legs in stockinette stitch for 1" (2.5cm).

Switch to CC on both legs. Work 4 rows in stockinette stitch.

Make Custom-Sized Shorts

1. Measure your toy's waist circumference, and divide the measurement by two: _____ (W)

2. Make a note of your gauge: _____ (G)

3. To calculate your cast-on, multiply the waist measurement by your gauge, and adjust the result to be a multiple of 4: (G) × (W) = _____ (CO)

Cast on according to your calculations, and work the instructions as written, adjusting the length of the shorts to fit your bear. When dividing for the legs, divide the stitches on the needle in half instead of the number listed in the pattern. Finish the pattern as written.

CUFFS

Switch to MC, work in k1, p1 rib for 4 rows on each leg. Bind off.

FINISHING

Sew Back to Front at sides and inseam. Weave in all ends.

With MC, crochet a 20" (50.8cm) chain. (page 13.) Thread through drawstring opening, and tie with a bow.

Sew on the number appliqué, using the photo as a guide.

HEADBAND

The headband is worked in a simple corrugated rib pattern.

Using MC, cast on 72 stitches.

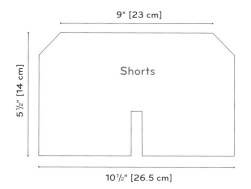

Shorts — 9" [23 cm], 5½" [14 cm], 10½" [26.5 cm]

Tip: When working this two-color ribbed pattern, always keep the unused yarn on the wrong side of the work.

Row 1 (RS) Attach CC and hold both strands of yarn to the back. K1 with CC, *bring MC to the front, p1 with MC, bring MC to the back, k1 with CC; repeat from * to the end of the row.

Row 2 (WS) *P1 with CC, bring MC to the back, k1, bring MC to the front; repeat from * to end.

Work **Rows 1 and 2** 4 times. Bind off.

Sew the cast-on row to the bind-off row to form a tube. Sew the side edges together to close the band.

Make a Custom-Sized Headband

1. Measure your toy's head circumference: _____ (H)

2. Make a note of your gauge: _____ (G)

3. Multiply your gauge by your head measurement. Add 1 stitch if necessary to get an even number: (G) × (H) = _____ (CO)

Cast on according to your calculations and follow the instructions as written in the main pattern.

PAPARAZZI GOWN, GLOVES, AND BAG

Pearl is ready for the red carpet in her glittering gown, complete with fur-trimmed gloves and evening bag. The halter-style dress is knit in one piece from the neck down. The bag and gloves are trimmed with glamorous Bamboo Feather yarn.

Special Stitches

S2KP: Slip 2 stitches at once as if to knit them together, knit 1, pass the slipped stitches over the stitch just knit.

Garter Stitch Lace Edging (multiple of 8 + 1)

Row 1 *K1, yo, ssk, k3, k2tog, yo; repeat from * to the last stitch, k1.

Row 2 Knit.

Row 3 *K2, yo, ssk, k1, k2tog, yo, k1; repeat from * to the last stitch, k1.

Row 4 Knit.

Row 5 *K3, yo, S2KP, yo, k2; repeat from * to the last stitch, k1.

GOWN

Cast on 18 stitches.
Begin halter increases: K1, kf&b, knit to end.

Repeat the halter increase row 17 times more—32 stitches.

Add Stitches for Back

Using cable cast-on, cast on 16 stitches—48 stitches.

Row 1 Knit to end of row; cast on 16 stitches—64 stitches.

Row 2 Knit.

SKIRT

Increase Row *K1, kf&b; repeat from * to last two stitches, end kf&b, kf&b—97 stitches. Work even in garter stitch for 4" (10cm), ending with a right-side row.

Work 5 rows of the Garter Lace Edging pattern (page 58).
Bind off.

FINISHING

Weave in all ends.

Skill Level

Beginner

Finished Measurements

Length: 7½" (19cm)

Waist: 18" (45.5cm)

Materials

2 skeins Lion Brand Glitterspun [60% acrylic, 27% cupro, 13% polyester, 115 yd (105m) per 1¾ oz (50g)], color: 990-144 Amethyst (MC), (4) medium

1 skein South West Trading Company Bamboo Feather [88% bamboo, 12% nylon; 109 yd (100m) per 3½ oz (100g)], color: 238 Purple (CC), (4) medium (CC)

Size 8 (5mm) circular needles, 24" (61cm) long or size needed to obtain gauge

Size 8 (5mm) double-pointed needles

Size 7 (4.5mm) crochet hook

Measuring tape

Yarn needle

Gauge

18 stitches and 26 rows per 4" (10 cm) in stockinette

HALTER STRAPS

Crochet 2 chains, each 24" (61cm) long. Attach one to each corner of the front halter portion of the dress. To wear, draw the chains behind the neck, cross them in back, wrap the chains around to the front waist, and cross again. Tie the chains in back.

FUR GLOVES

(Make 2)

With CC and double-pointed needles, cast on 28 stitches. Join to work in the round. Knit 2 rounds.

Switch to MC and knit 3½" (9cm).

Next round (decrease round) K2tog around—14 stitches.

Break the yarn, leaving a long tail. Thread the tail onto a tapestry needle and through all stitches; draw the stitches closed. Weave in all ends.

FUR PURSE

Work as for gloves up to (but not including) the decrease round.

Divide the stitches equally between two needles. With the knit side facing, work a three-needle bind-off (see Special Techniques, page 12). Weave in all ends, and then turn the bag inside out so that the reverse stockinette side is the public side of the purse.

STRAP

Crochet a chain 8" (20.5cm) long (page 11). Attach the ends to opposite sides of the purse, stitching on the inside of the purse.

Make Custom-Sized Gloves

1. Measure the circumference of your toy's arm: _____ (A)

2. Make a note of your gauge: _____ (G)

3. Multiply your gauge by the arm measurement: (G) x (A) = _____ (CO)

Cast on according to your calculations and follow the instructions as written, adjusting the length of the gloves to fit your bear.

Make a Custom-Sized Paparazzi Gown

1. Measure the front of your toy's chest between the shoulders: _____ (H)

2. Make note of your gauge: _____ (G)

3. Multiply the chest measurement by your gauge: (H) x (G) = _____ (CO)

Cast on the number specified and follow the pattern as written, working the increase portion only until the halter reaches the toy's "waist." Count the number of stitches on the needle and divide by 2: _____.

Cast on this number of stitches at the beginning of the next 2 rows for the skirt.

Continue following the main pattern at Begin Skirt, with the Increase Row.

Before beginning the Garter Lace Edging, work a lace setup row to add stitches and adjust the stitch count to be a multiple of 8 + 1 as necessary.

Finish the pattern as written.

GARTER LACE CHART

5			O	Λ	O					O	Λ	O						O	Λ	O				5
4	-	-	-	-	-	-	-	-	-	-	-	-	-	-	-	-	-	-	-	-	-	-	-	4
3			O	/		\	O			O	/		\	O				O	/		\	O		3
2	-	-	-	-	-	-	-	-	-	-	-	-	-	-	-	-	-	-	-	-	-	-	-	2
1	O	/			\	O		O	/			\	O		O	/			\	O				1

25 24 23 22 21 20 19 18 17 16 15 14 13 12 11 10 9 8 7 6 5 4 3 2 1

KEY

☐	Knit on rs, purl on ws
−	Purl on rs, knit on ws
\	ssk
/	K2tog
O	Yarn Over
Λ	Slip 2, K1, p2sso/slip2, p1,

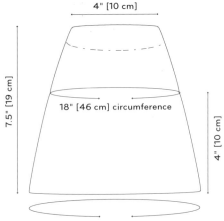

4" [10 cm]

7.5" [19 cm]

18" [46 cm] circumference

4" [10 cm]

24" [61 cm] circumference

Skill Level

Adventurous Beginner

Finished Measurements for Apron

Length, not including straps:
8½" (21.5cm)

Neck ties: 6" (15cm)

Waist ties: 8½" (21.5cm)

Width at neck: 4" (10cm)

Width below waistband: 5½" (14cm)

Finished Measurements for Hat

Circumference: 16" (40.5cm)

Height: 5½" (14cm) from cast on to the start of the crown

Materials

3 balls Peaches & Crème Double Worsted [100% cotton; 62 yd per 2½ oz], color: #1, white, (6) bulky

Note: 1 ball is needed for the apron, 2 balls for the chef's hat. To make the 2-color version, you'll need 4 balls—3 balls of color # 33, Persimmon (MC), and 1 ball of color # 51, Apple Green (CC).

Size 11 (8mm) circular knitting needles, 24" (61cm) long, or size needed to obtain gauge

Size 11 (8mm) double-pointed needles (optional, for finishing hat)

Measuring tape

Yarn needle

Gauge

12 stitches and 16 rows per 4" (10cm) in stockinette stitch

BEARS IN THE KITCHEN

Every bear needs his snack, whether it's elevenses or just a dip of hunny. This chef's hat and apron make sure the fur stays as clean as possible while the paws are in the pot.

Special Stitches

Seed Stitch: Alternate knits and purls in the first row (k1, p1, k1, p1 . . .), then knit the purls and purl the knits in following rows. Tip: If worked over an odd number, rows always begin with a knit stitch.

Lifted Right Increase (L-Rinc): Lift the right leg of the stitch below the stitch on the left needle, knit into that leg, then knit the stitch on the needle.

Lifted Left Increase (L-Linc): Knit the next stitch on the left needle, then insert the left needle into the left leg of the stitch two rows below the stitch on the right needle, knit into that leg.

Notes

To make a two-color apron, work the waistband, ties, and pocket in CC. To make a two-color hat, work the brim and the crown fold in CC.

As you are decreasing for the crown of the hat, you'll discover that the fabric is getting too small for your circular needle. When this happens, switch to double-pointed needles or simply pull the excess cord of the circular needle to make a loop poking out between the stitches, allowing you to continue to knit the small circumference. Move and re-create the loop as necessary—you might need one on each side at a time. (See Magic Loop, page 13.)

APRON

Cast on 13 stitches.

Row 1 (RS) *K1, p1; repeat from * to last stitch, end with k1.

Row 2 (WS) Repeat Row 1.

Row 3 K1, p1, knit to the last 2 stitches, p1, k1.

Row 4 K1, purl to the last stitch, k1. Repeat **Rows 3 and 4** until the apron measures 2" (5cm) from the cast-on edge, ending with a wrong-side (purl) row.

WAISTBAND AND TIES

Row 1 (RS) Work in seed stitch across the entire row. At the end of the row, cast on 26 stitches.

Row 2 (WS) Repeat Row 1.

Row 3 Work seed stitch across all 65 stitches.

Rows 4 and 5 Bind off 24 stitches, work in seed stitch to the end of the row—17 stitches.

POCKET

Row 1 K1, p1, knit to the last 2 stitches, p1, k1.

Row 2 K1, p1, purl to the last 2 stitches, p1, k1.

Row 3 K1, p1, k5, knit across 7 stitches for the pocket, turn.

Work back and forth in stockinette stitch across the 7 pocket stitches only until the pocket fabric measures 5" (12.5cm) long, ending with a wrong-side row. The pocket fabric will be folded in half to create a 2½" (6.5cm) pocket.

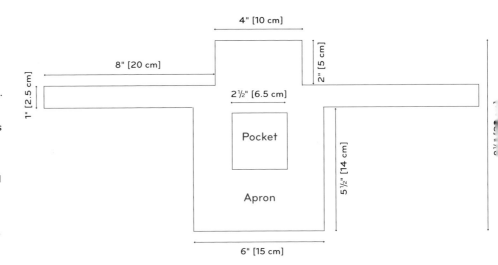

Finish Pocket

Row 1 (RS) Knit across the pocket stitches, fold the pocket in half toward the top of the apron, work in pattern across the rest of the apron stitches that remained unworked after the first row of the pocket.

Row 2 (WS) K1, p1, purl to the pocket stitches, knit across the pocket stitches (to create a purl bump fold), then purl to last 2 stitches, k1, p1.

Continue in stockinette stitch with a 2-stitch seed stitch border on each side of the apron until the apron measures 8" (20.5cm) from the cast-on edge.

Work 4 rows of seed stitch.

Bind off.

NECK STRAPS

With the right side facing, join yarn, and pick up 3 stitches at the right top edge of the apron's bib. Work these 3 stitches in seed stitch for 6" (15cm) to create a tie. Repeat at the left edge to create second tie.

FINISHING

Sew the sides of the pocket closed. Weave in all ends.

Make a Custom-Sized Apron

1. Measure the toy's front neck width: _____ (N)

2. Record your gauge (stitches per inch): _____ (G)

3. Multiply your gauge by the front neck width: (G) x (N) = _____ (W) (If your result is an even number, add 1 stitch.)

4. Add 4 stitches for the edging: (W) + 4 = _____ (CO)

Cast on according to your calculations. Follow the directions for the bib of the apron until your piece measures the distance from the bear's neck to its waist.

Adjust the number of stitches cast on for the ties if necessary. The **24** stitches suggested create 8½" (21cm) ties.

To work a pocket: If you've cast on a different number of stitches from the cast-on indicated in the main pattern, choose the number of stitches wide you'd like your pocket to be, and center them on your apron.

Finish the apron according to the main pattern instructions, adjusting the length to fit your bear as necessary.

CHEF'S HAT

Cast on 45 stitches.

BRIM

Rows 1–2 *K1, p1; repeat from * to the last stitch, k1.

Row 3 K1, p1, bind off 2 stitches for the buttonhole, work in seed stitch to the end of the row.

Row 4 Work in seed stitch to the last 2 stitches, cast on 2 stitches, p1, k1.

Row 5 Repeat Row 1.

PLEATS

Row 1 (RS) *K3, p2; repeat from * to the end of the row.

Row 2 Work the stitches as they appear (knit the knits and purl the purls), creating a rib pattern.

Row 3 *Place marker, work a lifted right increase in the next stitch, k2, p2; repeat from * to end.

Row 4 Work even, maintaining the rib pattern.

Increase as set after each marker on every right-side row for 3" (7.5cm), or until the hat is 1" (2.5cm) above the head and ears. At the end of the next right-side row, do not turn. Join to work in the round.

Maintain the rib pattern without increasing for 1" (2.5cm).

CROWN FOLD

Purl one round to create a clean fold for the crown of the hat.

Begin crown decreases

On the next round, *knit to 2 stitches before marker, k2tog, slip marker; repeat from * around. Repeat this round until there are only 2 stitches between each set of markers.

Cut the yarn, leaving a 15" (38cm) tail. Thread the yarn onto a yarn needle and slip the remaining stitches from the knitting needle to the yarn. Draw the stitches together to close the circle. Thread the needle down into the inside of the hat and secure. Weave in all ends.

Make a Custom-Sized Chef's Hat

1. Measure the toy's head circumference at the point where you'd like the hat to sit—be sure to go around the ears, too, if necessary: _____ (H)

2. Make a note of your gauge (stitches per inch/cm): _____ (G)

3. Add 1" (2.5cm) to the head circumference to allow for a buttonhole:
    (N) + (G)= _____ (I)

4. Multiply the result by your gauge, and adjust your result to be a multiple of 3: (I) × (G) _____ (CO)

Cast on according to your calculations and follow the instructions for the brim.

Setup for knit pleats
Count your stitches. Work one row, decreasing evenly as necessary across the row to arrive at a stitch count that's a multiple of 5.

Finish the hat as written in the pattern instructions.

Bears in Winter

Winter is a teddy's favorite season. When it's cold enough, even a furry bear wants a warm sweater or jacket. Mohair keeps Pearl warm in the Soft Sunrise Poncho (page 73). Eddie sports a traditional Fair Isle Sweater (page 75), and Joey hunts for firewood in his Fur-Trimmed Hoodie (page 64) and gets ready for a snowball fight in his Winter Hiking Set (page 69), a vest with matching ear flap hat and mittens.

FUR-TRIMMED HOODIE

When he's out gathering wood or out to play, Joey keeps warm with his faux (of course!) Fur-Trimmed Hoodie. Knit in one piece from the hood down, this jacket features hook-and-eye closures, a generous hood that looks great up or down, and two unusual yarns: a bamboo (faux) fur and a corn-based knitted tape.

HOOD

Cast on 66 stitches.
Work in stockinette stitch for 5" (12.5cm), ending with a wrong-side row.

Begin the hood decreases

On the next right-side row, k2, ssk, knit to last 4 stitches, k2tog, k2.
Repeat this row every right-side row until you have 58 stitches.
Work even until the hood measures 7" (18cm) from the cast-on edge, ending with a right-side row.

Set-up for the raglan increases and neck shaping

On the next wrong-side row, k3 (garter edging), p6, place marker, p1, place marker, p9, place marker, p1, place marker, p18, place marker, p1, place marker, p9, place marker, p1, place marker, p6, k3.

Begin the raglan increases and the neckline increases

Row 1 (RS) K3, kf&b, *knit to 1 stitch before marker, kf&b, slip marker, k1, slip marker, kf&b; repeat from * to last 4 stitches, kf&b, k3.
Row 2 K3, purl to last 3 stitches, k3.

Repeat **Rows 1–2** twice more, and then continue the raglan increases as follows:

Row 1 (RS) K3, *knit to 1 stitch before marker, kf&b, slip marker, k1, slip marker, kf&b; repeat from * to last 3 stitches, k3.
Row 2 K3, purl to last 3 stitches, k3.

Repeat **Rows 1–2** until there are 38 stitches between the sleeve markers, or the sleeve measures 7" (18cm) across.

Skill Level

Intermediate

Finished Measurements

Hood: 7" (18cm)

Chest Circumference: 18" (45.5cm)

Length: 5¼" (13.5cm)

Sleeve: 7" (18cm), from neck to cuff

Materials

2 skeins South West Trading Company A-MAIZing [100% corn fiber; 142 yd (130m) per 1¾ oz (50g)], color: 372 khaki (MC), light

1 skein South West Trading Company Bamboo Feather [88% Bamboo, 12% nylon; 109 yd (100m) per 3½ oz (100g)], color: 240 taupe (CC), medium

Size 8 (5mm) needles, or size needed to obtain gauge

8 stitch markers

Hook-and-eye closures

Sewing thread and needle

Measuring tape

Yarn needle

Gauge

22 stitches and 31 rows per 4" (10 cm) in stockinette

Place the sleeve stitches on holders

On the next right-side row, knit to the 1st marker, place the stitches between the 1st and 3rd markers on a holder for the left sleeve, cast on 2 stitches for the underarm, knit to the 6th marker, place the stitches between the 6th and last markers on a holder for the right sleeve, cast on 2 stitches for the underarm, knit to the end of the row. Remove all markers as you come to them in the next row.

Work even on the body stitches until the sweater measures 3¼" (8cm) from the center back neck, or 10" (25.5cm) from the cast-on edge.

Change to CC. Work 5 rows in garter stitch. Bind off.

SLEEVES

Slip stitches for the first sleeve onto the working needle. Work 5 rows in stockinette stitch with MC. Change to CC. Work 3 rows in garter stitch. Bind off.
Repeat the instructions for the second sleeve.

FINISHING

Sew the underarm seams.

Fold the hood in half, and sew the cast-on edge closed.

HOOD EDGING

Using CC, pick up and knit 3 stitches for every 4 rows around the hood opening. Knit 5 rows in garter stitch for the fur edging. Bind off.

Tack down the corners of the fur edging, if desired, to bring the edging in line with the jacket opening.

Weave in all ends.

Sew on the hook-and-eye closures.

Make a Custom-Sized Hooded Sweater

1. Measure the back of the toy's neck and record that measurement here: _____ (N)

2. Record your gauge: _____ (G)

3. Multiply your gauge by your key measurement: (G) x (N) = _____ (N1)

4. Take the result and multiply that by 2 to add sleeve stitches: (N1) x (2) = _____ (N2)

5. The raglan increases surround four "seam" stitches, which help to mark the increase and give a decorative look to the garment. These stitches need to be added to your cast-on. The result is the number needed for your neckline: (N2) + 4 = _____ (K)

6. Calculate Arm Stitches: (N1) ÷ 2 = _____ (A)

7. Subtract your garter stitch edging (3 stitches) from Arm Stitches to get your front stitches: (A) – 3 = _____ (F)

8. Add 10 stitches to (K) to get the cast-on number for the hood: _____ (CO)

Cast on according to your calculations. Follow the instructions for knitting the hood. Work the decreases until you're back down to your neckline calculation (K).

Use your back neck stitch count (N1) as a guide for placing the markers.

Set up for the raglan increases
On the next wrong-side row, k3, p (F), place marker, p1, place marker, p (A), place marker, p1, place marker, p (N1), place marker, p1, place marker, p (A), place marker, p1, place marker, p (F), k3.

Follow the main pattern, beginning with the first raglan increase row. Be sure to work raglan increases only until the sleeve portion of your sweater wraps comfortably around the bear's arm, then continue from "Place sleeve stitches on holders."

Finish the main pattern as written.

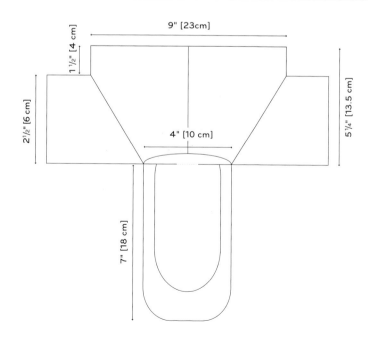

WINTER HIKING SET

Adventurous Beginner

Finished Measurements

Width: 8" (20.5cm)

Height: 4½" (11.5cm) (shoulder to hem)

Armhole Depth: 3" (7.5cm)

Back Neck Width: 4½" (11.5cm)

V-Neck Depth: 2½" (6.5cm)

Materials

1 skein Nature's Palette [90% Organic Wool, 10% Mohair; 230 yd (205m) per 4 oz (113g)], color: NP-133 Dark Teal (MC), (4) medium

1 skein Nature's Palette [90% Organic Wool, 10% Mohair; 230 yd (205m) per 4 oz (113g)], color: NP-122 Spring Grass (CC), (4) medium

Size 9 (5.5mm) knitting needles, or size needed to obtain gauge

Size 9 (5.5mm) circular or double pointed knitting needles (for mittens)

Size 5 (3.75mm) circular knitting needles (for vest edgings)

Measuring tape

Yarn needle

Yarn Note: Spool a second small ball of dark teal from the main ball before beginning to have it ready to work the V-neck and shoulder (which require two balls at once).

Gauge

15 stitches and 22 rows = 4" (10cm) in stockinette stitch

When Joey is out to play on a winter's day, he keeps warm in his Winter Hiking Set. Paws and ears are protected with the earflap hat and cozy mittens. Both match the vest, which features simple colorwork and contrasting finishing details. The hat and mittens are knit in the round, while the vest is worked flat in two pieces.

Special Stitches

Mosaic Band

This vest, hat, and mittens set features a small band of color work called "mosaic knitting," or slip stitch patterning. In mosaic knitting, only one color is worked in each row. The pattern appears because the stitches in the contrasting color in that row are slipped with the yarn held to the wrong side of the work. The simple check pattern used in this set is worked as follows:

Row 1 (RS) With CC, *k2, slip 2 stitches with yarn in back; repeat from *to the last 2 stitches, k2.

Row 2 (WS) With CC, *p2, slip 2 stitches with yarn in front; repeat from * to the last 2 stitches, p2.

When the pattern is worked in the round (as for the mittens), work **Row 2** the same as **Row 1**.

Two-Color Long-Tail Cast-On

To get the contrasting color edge used in these patterns, work a long-tail cast-on with one strand of MC and one strand of CC. The CC yarn should be over your thumb. That way, the edge will be in the contrasting color, and the stitches on the needle will be in the main color.

VEST
BACK

Using the two-color long-tail cast-on and larger needles, cast on 30 stitches.
Drop CC and begin k2, p2 rib with MC only.

Rows 1 and 3 *P2, k2; repeat from * to last 2 stitches, p2.

Rows 2 and 4 *K2, p2; repeat from * to last 2 stitches, k2.

Work in stockinette stitch until the piece measures 1½" (4cm) from the cast-on edge, ending with a wrong-side row.
Work the two rows of the Mosaic Band, then shape armholes.

Begin armhole shaping
Row 1 (RS) K2, ssk, knit to last 3 stitches, k2tog, k2.
Row 2 Purl.

Repeat these 2 rows 3 more times. Work even until the piece measures 3½" (9cm) from the cast-on edge, ending with a wrong-side row.

Shape the neck
Row 1 (RS) K5, bind off 12 stitches, k5.
Row 2 P5, join a second ball of yarn to the other shoulder. Work in stockinette stitch on both shoulders until the piece measures 4½" (11.5cm) from the cast-on edge. Slip the stitches to holders. Set Back aside.

FRONT
Work as for Back up to and including the first 2 rows of armhole shaping.

Begin the V-neck shaping, maintaining armhole shaping
Divide the stitches in half and mark the center of the row.
Row 1 (RS) K2, ssk, knit to 3 stitches before the marker, k2tog, k1; join a second ball of yarn to work both sides of V-neck at once, and with second ball, k1, ssk, knit to 4 stitches before the end of the row, k2tog, k2.
Row 2 Purl.
Rows 3–6 Work as for **Rows 1** and **2**.
Row 7 Knit to 3 stitches before the neck opening, k2tog, k1; with the second ball,

---

Make a Custom-Sized Winter Vest

1. Measure your toy's chest/belly circumference at the widest point and divide the measurement in half: _____ (B)

2. Make a note of your gauge _____ (G)

3. Multiply (G) x (B) and adjust the result so that you have an even number _____ (CO)

Cast on for the Back according to your calculations, and follow the instructions as written. When you bind off for the back neck, instead of 12, subtract 10 from the number of stitches on the needles and use that number as your Back Neck bind-off.

Sizing Notes
If your toy is much bigger than 18" (45cm) tall, you may want to make the vest longer. Add length by working even before the armhole shaping (right after the mosaic band). Similarly, if your toy has very large arms, you can increase the size of the armholes by working even for a few more rows after you finish the armhole shaping. Just be sure to carry any length adjustments through to the front piece.

Tip: If you're making a vest for a very small bear, consider working the pattern as written in a DK or lighter yarn on smaller needles, depending on gauge.

---

k1, ssk, knit to the end of the row.
Row 8 Purl.

Repeat **Rows 7 and 8** until 5 stitches remain on each side. Work even in stockinette stitch until the Front measures 4½" (11.5cm). Do not bind off.

FINISHING

Join Front and Back at the shoulders
Slide the shoulder stitches from the Back onto the second needle. Holding the Front and Back parallel with right sides together, use a spare needle to join the shoulders using a three-needle bind-off (page 12).

ARMHOLE RIBBING
Using smaller needles and CC, pick up stitches evenly across the armhole opening on the first side, from underarm edge to underarm edge. Work 2 rows of k1, p1 rib. Bind off in rib. Repeat for the second side.

V-NECK RIBBING
The neckline is worked in the round. Beginning at the center back, with the smaller needles and CC, pick up stitches evenly around the neck opening. Mark the stitch at the center front of the V.

Join at the back to work in the round.

70   Bears in Winter

Rounds 1–2 Work in k1, p1 rib to 1 stitch before the marked center stitch; slip 2, k1, psso (two stitches decreased), continue in rib to the end of the round.

Bind off in rib.

Weave in ends.

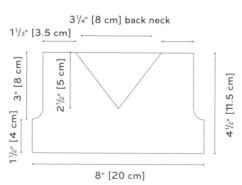

3¼" [8 cm] back neck

1⅓" [3.5 cm]

3" [8 cm]

2½" [5 cm]

1½" [4 cm]

4½" [11.5 cm]

8" [20 cm]

WINTER HAT

Using the two-color long-tail cast-on and double-pointed needles, cast on 64 stitches. Join to work in the round.

With MC, work in k2, p2 rib for 3 rounds.

Work in stockinette stitch for 3 rounds.

Work the two-row Mosaic Band.

Work 2 rounds in stockinette stitch.

Begin Crown Decreases

Setup Round *K8, place marker; repeat from * around (8 markers placed).
Round 1 *Knit to 2 stitches before marker, k2tog; repeat from * around (8 stitches decreased).
Round 2 Knit.
Repeat these 2 rounds 5 more times—16 stitches remaining.
Final Round K2tog around.
Cut yarn, leaving a long tail. Thread end through a yarn needle and draw the needle through the remaining 8 live stitches. Draw crown closed and fasten off. Weave in ends.

EARFLAPS

Choose 11 stitches on one side of the hat for the first ear flap, and set them off with markers. Center the second flap directly opposite the first and set the stitches off with markers.
With the wrong side facing, pick up the first set of 11 stitches marked off just above the contrasting cast-on row.

Make a Custom-Sized Winter Hat

Multiply your toy's head circumference by your gauge and adjust the result to a multiple of 8: _____ (CO).

Cast on according to your calculations and follow the instructions as written, working more or fewer decrease rounds if necessary. If your toy's head is very small, you'll probably want smaller earflaps. Just pick up fewer stitches and follow the main instructions. Work even for a short bit, decrease on each side twice, and bind off.

Row 1 (RS) Knit.
Row 2 K2, purl to last 2 stitches, k2.
Repeat these 2 rows 4 more times.

Flap Decreases

Row 1 (RS) K3, ssk, knit to last 5 stitches, k2tog, k3.
Row 2 K2, purl to last 2 stitches, k2.
Row 3 K3, k3tog, k3.
Bind off.
Repeat the instructions for the second flap.

MITTENS

(Make 2)
Using two-color long-tail cast-on and double-pointed needles (page 13), cast on 24 stitches. Join to work in the round.
Rounds 1–4 Work in k2, p2 rib.
Rounds 5–8 Knit.

Make Custom-Sized Mittens

1. Measure your toy's wrist circumference: _____ (W).

2. Make a note of your gauge: _____ (G).

3. Multiply the wrist circumference by the gauge: (G) x (W) = _____.

4. Adjust the result to be a multiple of 2: _____ (CO).

Cast on according to your calculations. Work the pattern as written, adjusting the length to fit your needs.

Tip: If you want mittens with thumbs, slip a few stitches onto a holder where you'd like the thumb to go, and cast that same number back on in the next round. After finishing the mitten, slide the "parked" stitches onto a needle, pick up stitches around the thumb opening, join to work in the round, and knit the thumb.

Rounds 9 and 10 Work the two-row Mosaic Band.
Rounds 11–14 Knit.
Decrease Round *K2, k2tog; repeat from * around.
Divide the remaining 12 stitches between 2 needles. Flip the mitten to the wrong side. Work three-needle bind off (page 12). Fasten off. Weave in ends.

SOFT SUNRISE LACY PONCHO

Pearl's lacy poncho is light and airy and provides just the touch of warmth a bear needs in a winter wonderland. Knit in a silk and mohair laceweight yarn, the poncho consists of two identical lace panels sewn at right angles to create a triangular shape.

Skill Level

Intermediate

Finished Measurements

Each panel measures 4³/₄" (12cm) wide by 12" (30.5cm) long.

Materials

1 skein Knit One Crochet Too Douceur et Soie [65% baby mohair, 35% silk; 225 yd (205m) per ³/₄ oz (25g)], color: 8243 soft sunrise, (2) fine

Size 5 (3.75mm) knitting needles, or size needed to obtain gauge

Measuring tape

Yarn needle

Gauge

23 stitches and 40 rows = 4" (10cm) in pattern.

To make a gauge swatch, cast on the required stitches for the poncho and work in pattern for 4–5" (11–12.5cm). The piece should block to 4³/₄" (12cm) wide. Gauge can be approximate for this pattern, so if you're close, you can keep going.

Special Stitch

S2KP Slip 2 stitches at once as if to k2tog, k1, pass both slipped stitches over the stitch just knit.

Stitch Pattern

Simple Eyelet Rib

Worked over a multiple of 5 stitches plus 2

Row 1 (RS) S1, *p2, k3; repeat from * to the last stitch, k1.

Row 2 (WS) S1, *p3, k2; repeat from * to the last stitch, p1.

Rows 3 and 4 Repeat Rows 1 and 2.

Row 5 S1, *k2, yo, s2kp, yo; repeat from * to the last stitch, k1.

Row 6 Repeat **Row 2**.

PONCHO

(Make 2 panels.)

Cast on 27 stitches.

Work in Simple Eyelet Rib for 12" (30.5cm).

Bind off.

FINISHING

Block pieces to measurements.

ASSEMBLY

With right sides facing, place one short edge of the first piece along one long edge of the second piece, making sure that the corners align. Sew from the corner to the end of the short edge. Repeat the process with the short edge of the second piece and the long edge of the first piece. (Use the photograph as a guide).

Weave in all ends.

Make a Custom-Sized Poncho

Pearl's Soft Sunrise Poncho will easily fit a variety of toys. If you're knitting for a very large or a very small toy, the best way to determine the size of your rectangular panel is to make a paper pattern of the poncho you'd like to make.

1. Make a gauge swatch using the yarn and needles you've chosen.

2. Cut out two paper rectangles and tape them together following the finishing instructions. Try the paper poncho on your toy and make adjustments to achieve your desired fit and size.

3. When the paper pieces are the right size, measure the pieces, and lay your gauge swatch on top of one of the panels to estimate how many repeats of the lace pattern you'd like to add or remove.

Cast on according to your calculations and knit until your piece measures the length of your paper pattern. Repeat for the second piece, and finish according to the instructions in the main pattern.

LACE CHART

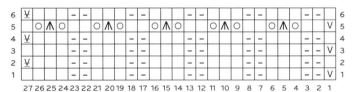

KEY

☐	Knit on RS, purl on WS
–	Purl on RS, knit on WS
O	Yarn Over
⋀	Slip 2, K1, p2sso/slip2, p1
V	Slip 1
⋎	Slip 1 w/yarn in front

Skill Level

Experienced

Finished Measurements

Circumference: 14" (35.5cm)

Length: 6" (15cm)

Sleeve length: 5" (12.5cm)

Materials

Yarns International Shetland 2000 [100% Shetland wool; 190 yd (174m) per 1³⁄₄ oz (50g)], (**1**) super fine

Color A: 1 skein Shetland Black

Color B: 1 skein Sholmit

Color C: 1 skein Gaulmgot

Color D: 1 skein Yuglet

Color E: 1 skein Shetland White

Size 4 (3.25mm) circular needle, 16" (40cm), or size needed to obtain gauge

Size 4 (3.25mm) double-pointed needles

2 stitch markers

5 stitch holders (or lengths of scrap yarn)

1 button, ¹⁄₂" (13mm) diameter

Note: Due to the complexity of the colorwork, this pattern is offered only in the standard 16–18" (40.5–45.5cm) bear size. To vary the size of the sweater, consider changing needle sizes and yarn weight.

Gauge

25 stitches and 32 rows = 4" (10cm) in Fair Isle pattern

BY SPECIAL GUEST DESIGNER JENNIFER WOODS

Eddie's favorite Fair Isle is patterned with hearts that resemble teddy faces. This beautiful, traditional Fair Isle sweater, worked in the round, is knit with five shades of undyed Shetland wool—the colors come straight from the sheep! Designer Jennifer Woods has given step-by-step instructions for first-time Fair Isle knitters, as well as a detailed introduction to the technique, so why not use this small sweater as an introduction to Fair Isle knitting?

BODY

With Color A and the circular needle, cast on 92 stitches. Place marker and join in the round, being careful not to twist. Note that round numbers in the pattern correspond to round numbers on the chart (page 78).

Round 1 Knit.

Round 2 Join Color B; *with A, k2, with B, k2; repeat from * to end.

Rounds 3, 4, and 5 *with A, k2, with B, p2; repeat from * to end.

Round 6 With A, knit.

Round 7 With A, purl. Cut Color A, leaving a tail to weave in later.

Round 8 Join Color E, and knit, placing a marker after 46 stitches to mark second side seam.

Rounds 9–21 Follow chart.

ARMHOLE AND STEEK SET-UP

Round 22 Slip the first 2 stitches onto a holder, follow the Chart to 2 stitches before the marker place marker, slip the next 4 stitches onto a holder; cast on 6 stitches for the steek, place marker, follow the chart to 2 stitches before the marker, slip 2 stitches onto the holder with 2 stitches from the start of the round; cast on 6 stitches for the steek.

Rows 23–44 Continue following the chart, working the steek stitches as follows: On one-colored rows, simply knit the stitches in that color. On two-colored rows, alternate colors each stitch, creating a checkerboard effect. For instance, 1 round will be worked C, D, C, D, C, D and the next will be worked D, E, D, E, D, E.

Introduction to Fair Isle Knitting

Classic Fair Isle knitting, worked with two colors per row, is just like knitting stockinette stitch in the round, except for the fact that you have to manage two strands of yarn. Following the chart, one color is used to knit the stitch and the second is carried loosely behind the just-made stitch. Be mindful that the strand of yarn, called a "float," is not pulled too tightly, as this will cause puckering. At this gauge, if the float spans three stitches, it should be about ½" (13mm) long, as three stitches are ½" (13mm) wide. Knitters who are comfortable with both English style and Continental style knitting can carry one color with their right hand and one with their left; others will prefer to carry the two colors of yarn in one hand. Use whichever technique works best for you.

Corrugated ribbing is ribbing worked in two colors. One color is used for the knit stitches and the other for the purl stitches. All yarn is held to the wrong side when not in use.

A Fair Isle technique that may be new to you is steeking. Steeks allow you to knit things such as sweaters without interrupting the pattern to create neck or armhole openings. This allows you to work the whole piece in the round. After completing the tube, a straight line is cut along a column of stitches, creating an opening. The steek itself is a bridge of extra stitches where the cut is made and is usually 6–10 stitches wide.

While steeks can be worked in any yarn, wool works best for steeks, particularly Shetland wool. Its short staple length means that the strands of yarn can "grab" onto one another, making it difficult for them to unravel easily.

After the steek is cut, the edges are tacked down on the wrong side of the fabric to create a neat edge. After a garment with steeks has been worn and washed a few times, the facings will full and become durable finishes on the inside of the garment.

FRONT NECK AND STEEK

Round 45 Work the first 10 stitches according to the chart, slip the next 22 stitches onto a holder, place marker, cast on 6 steek stitches, place marker, and work the rest of the round according to the chart.

Round 46 On the front, work to 2 stitches before the marker, k2tog, work 6 steek stitches, slip marker, ssk, work the rest of the round according to chart.

Round 47 Work as charted.

Round 48 Repeat the decreases as for Round 46.

Round 49 Work as charted.

Round 50 Bind off the first 3 steek stitches; work chart to neck steek, bind off 6 steek stitches; work to the armhole steek, bind off 6 steek stitches; work the last 3 steek stitches, bind off 3 stitches. Place the first 8 stitches on a holder for lef front shoulder; place the next 8 stitches for the right front shoulder on a double-pointed needle; place the 8 stitches of the right back shoulder on a double-pointed needle; place the center 24 stitches of the back neck on a holder, and place the last 8 stitches on a holder for the left back shoulder.

Cutting Steeks

There are three steeks to cut—one for each armhole and one for the neck. Cut between the 3rd and 4th stitch of each steek. Don't worry about finishing the steeks at this point; the nature of Shetland wool is to stick together.

RIGHT SHOULDER

Turn the sweater inside out. Hold the two double-pointed needles with 8 stitches each for the Right Shoulder parallel in your left hand and work the three-needle bind-off (page 12) to attach the shoulder.

LEFT SHOULDER

Turn the sweater right-side out. Slip the 8 stitches for the left front shoulder onto a double-pointed needle and attach Color A. Work 4 rows in k2, p2 rib.
Bind off.
Slip the 8 stitches for the left back shoulder onto a double-pointed needle and attach Color A.

Work 2 rows in k2, p2 ribbing.
Make a buttonhole as follows
Row 1 K2, p1, bind off 2 stitches, k1, p2.

Row 2 K2, p1, cast on 2 stitches, K1, p2. Work 1 more row in rib, then bind off in pattern.

NECKBAND

Baste the buttonhole bands from the left shoulder together to make it easier to pick up stitches for the left sleeve and the neckband.

With Color A and the circular needle, starting at left front edge, pick up and knit 4 stitches to the front neck holder, knit the 22 stitches from the front neck holder, pick up and knit 4 stitches to shoulder seam on the right shoulder, knit the 24 stitches from the back neck holder—54 stitches.
Working back and forth, work 3 rows in k2, p2 rib.
Bind off in rib.

SLEEVES

(Make 2)

With A and double-pointed needles, start at the center of the 4 underarm stitches, and pick up and knit 56 stitches around the sleeve openings as follows: pick up and knit 2 stitches from underarm, 26 stitches to the shoulder seam, 26 stitches from shoulder seam to underarm, and 2 stitches from underarm—56 stitches.
Place marker and join in the round.

Work the 43 rows of the sleeve chart, reading from top to bottom.
Bind off with Color A.

FINISHING

Weave in any loose ends. Remove basting stitches. Steam block the sweater and allow to dry. Sew the button on the left front shoulder placket.

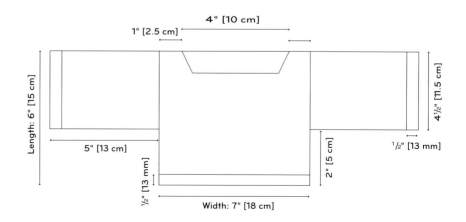

KEY

◆	Shetland Black	✛	Yuglet
▣	Sholmit	O	Shetland White
☐	Gaulmogot		

Bedtime for Bears

At the end of the day, Pearl and Eddie like to get cozy in their organic cotton bedclothes. Both outfits feature Henley-style neck openings with pearl buttons. Eddie's Jammies (page 85) are complete with feet, while Pearl's nightgown (page 80) has a vintage feel with embroidered flowers and crocheted edgings. Joey stays warm after his bath in the Fuzzy Wuzzy Bathrobe (page 89).

FLORAL NIGHTGOWN

At bedtime, Pearl relaxes in her pretty-in-pink nightgown. Full of vintage-inspired details, the nightgown features pearl buttons, a simple crocheted edging, and small embroidered flowers scattered about the skirt.

BODY

With MC, cast on 58 stitches.

Rows 1–3 K2, *k1, p1; repeat from * to last 2 stitches, k2.

Set up for the raglan increases

On the next wrong-side row, k2 (garter edging), p7, place marker, p1, place marker, p9, place marker, p1, place marker, p18, place marker, p1, place marker, p9, place marker, p1, place marker, p7, k2.

Begin the raglan increases and work buttonholes

Row 1 (RS) K3, yo, k2tog, *knit to 1 stitch before the marker, kf&b, slip marker, k1, slip marker, kf&b; repeat from * 3 times, knit to the end of the row.

Row 2 (WS) K2, purl to the last 2 stitches, k2.

Row 3 Knit to 1 stitch before the marker, kf&b, slip marker, k1, slip marker, kf&b; repeat from * 3 times, knit to the end of the row.

Row 4 Repeat **Row 2**.

Repeat **Rows 1–4** 3 times more.

Create henley opening

Slip the last 5 stitches from the end without buttonholes to a spare double-pointed or circular needle. These stitches will become the button band. Hold the piece to join in the round with the right side facing, overlapping the first and last 5 stitches so that the buttonholes are on top. Work the three-needle non-bind-off (page 13) over 3 stitches, place a different-colored marker to note the beginning of the round; finish the non-bind-off over the next 2 stitches, and then continue knitting in the round as directed below.

Note: The join may create a small gap at the bottom edge of the button band. This can be sewn closed from the wrong side during finishing.

Skill Level

Intermediate

Finished Measurements

Chest Circumference: 18" (45.5cm)

Length: 10" (25.5cm)

Sleeve: 6" (15cm) from neck to cuff

Materials

2 skeins Bernat Organic Cotton [100% organic cotton; 87 yd (80m) per 1³⁄₄ oz (50g)], color: 43426 prairie rose (MC), (4) medium

2 skeins Bernat Organic Cotton [100% organic cotton; 87 yd (80m) per 1³⁄₄ oz (50g)], color: 43006 muslin (CC), (4) medium

Size 7 (4.5mm) circular needles, 24" (61cm), or size needed to obtain gauge

Size 7 double-pointed needles (optional)

Four small shank buttons

Size 7 (4.5mm) crochet hook

Measuring tape

Yarn needle

8 stitch markers

Gauge

19 stitches and 28 rows = 4" (10 cm) in stockinette stitch

Continue the raglan increases

Round 1 (RS) *Knit to 1 stitch before the marker, kf&b, slip marker, k1, slip marker, kf&b; repeat from * 3 times, knit to the end of the round.
Round 2 Knit.

Repeat **Rounds 1 and 2** until the sleeve portion of the sweater measures 7" (18cm) across (measure between the increases). End after a **Round 2**.

Place sleeve stitches on holders

Knit to the first raglan marker, place the sleeve stitches (up to the third marker) on a holder, removing markers, cast on 2 stitches under the arm, knit to the sixth marker, place the stitches for the second sleeve on a holder (up to the eighth marker), cast on 2 stitches under the arm, knit to the end of the round.

Begin the darts for the skirt

To set up, count your stitches and mark the center back of the round. Your original round marker will denote the center front.

From the beginning of round marker, k7, place marker, k1, place marker, knit to 8 stitches before the center back marker, place marker, k1, place marker, knit to the center back marker and remove it, k7, place marker, k1, place marker, knit to 8 stitches before the center front marker, place

marker, k1, place marker, knit to the end of the round, and remove the center front marker.

Round 1 *Knit to 1 stitch before the marker, kf&b, slip marker, k1, slip marker, kf&b; repeat from * 3 times, knit to end of round.
Round 2 Knit.

Make a Custom-Sized Nightgown

1. Measure the back of the toy's neck and record that measurement here: _____ (N)

2. Record your gauge: _____ (G)

3. Multiply your gauge by your neck measurement: (G) x (N) = _____ (N1)

4. Take the result and multiply it by 2 to add sleeve stitches: (N1) x 2 = _____ (N2)

5. Add Seam Stitches: The raglan increases surround four "seam" stitches, which help to mark the increase and give a decorative look to the garment. Add these stitches to calculate the correct cast-on number:
(N2) + 4 = _____ (CO)

6. Calculate arm stitches,
(N1) ÷ 2 = _____ (A)

7. Subtract your button band stitches from the arm stitches to get your front stitches: A - 2 = _____ (F)

Cast on according to your calculations and set up for the raglan increases as follows:

Use your back neck stitch count (N1) as a guide for placing the markers.

Row 1 Knit the garter edge, k(F), place marker, k1, place marker, k(A), place marker, k1, place marker, k(N1), place marker, k1, place marker, k(A), place marker, k1, place marker, k(F), knit the garter edge.

Follow the main pattern starting with **Begin raglan increases and buttonholes**.

Notes
Work the raglan increases until the arm portion of the sweater can wrap comfortably around your toy's arm. If you're knitting for a very small toy, you may want to work fewer buttonholes. Adjust the length of the arms and skirt as well as the placement of the darts to fit your toy.

Repeat these 2 rounds 7 times more (64 stitches added). If you'd like a less full skirt, you can stop the darts earlier.

Knit even for 3" (7.5cm).

Bind off.

SLEEVES

Slip the stitches from the first sleeve back onto a size 7 circular or double-pointed needle; pick up 2 stitches under the arm, and join to work in the round.

Work even in stockinette stitch for 3" (7.5cm). Repeat for the second sleeve.

Bind off.

FINISHING

Sew up any gaps and weave in ends. Sew on buttons underneath the buttonholes.

CROCHETED SLEEVE EDGING

Using CC and a size 7 (4.5mm) crochet hook, single crochet evenly around both cuffs. Fasten off.

CROCHETED SKIRT EDGING

(For crochet help, see page 11).
Round 1 Using CC and a size 7 (4.5mm) crochet hook, begin at center back and sc evenly around the skirt hem.
Round 2 Ch 3, *skip 2 stitches, work 3 dc (shell) in the next stitch; repeat from * around. Fasten off.

EMBROIDERY

The floral embroidery is a combination of French knots and a simple petal stitch. To work the flower, using yarn needle and CC, work a French knot where you'd like

the center of the flower to be. To create the petals, bring the needle up to the right side of the fabric next to the French knot and back down very close to where you brought it up, leaving a loop about ½" (13mm) long showing. Tack down the center of the loop with a small stitch to create the petal shape. Work three petals for each flower. You can work any number of flowers on the skirt. Use the photo as a guide for placement. Weave in ends.

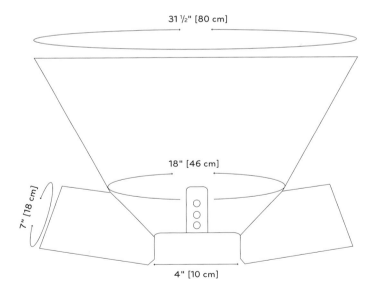

31 ½" [80 cm]

18" [46 cm]

7" [18 cm]

4" [10 cm]

STORYTIME STRIPES FOOTIE PAJAMAS

When the day is done, Eddie likes nothing better than to snuggle into his PJs. This pair matches Pearl's Vintage Floral nightgown with the Henley closure and pearl buttons, but features a striped body and solid sleeves for a layered look, ribbed cuffs, and, of course, footies.

Skill Level

Intermediate

Finished Measurements

Chest Circumference: 18½" (47cm)

Length: 15" (38cm) from shoulder to footie bottom

Sleeve: 6" (15cm) from neck to cuff

Materials

2 skeins Bernat Organic Cotton [100% organic cotton; 87 yd (80m) per 1¾ oz (50g)], color: 43116 mineral spring (MC), (4) medium

2 skeins Bernat Organic Cotton [100% organic cotton; 87 yd (80m) per 1¾ oz (50g)], color: 43117 oasis (CC), (4) medium

Size 7 (4.5mm) circular needles, or size needed to obtain gauge

Size 7 double-pointed needles (optional)

Three ⅜" (2cm) shank buttons

Measuring tape

Yarn needle

8 stitch markers

2 stitch holders, or lengths of scrap yarn

Gauge

19 stitches and 28 rows = 4" (10 cm) in stockinette stitch

Stripe Sequence

In this pattern the MC and CC yarns are striped in the yoke, the body, and the legs of the Jammies, changing colors every two rows. (For the model, I worked the sleeves from elbow to cuff in the MC, but you could stripe that part, too.) After you join the work in the round, be sure to carry the non-working color up the wrong side of the work.

NECK

With MC, cast on 58 stitches.
Rows 1–2 K2, *k1, p1; repeat from * to last two stitches, end with k2.
Row 3 Change to CC, and repeat **Row 1**. Continue to change colors every two rows.

Set up for raglan increases

Next Row (WS) K2 (garter edging), p7, place marker, p1, place marker, p9, place marker, p1, place marker, p18, place marker, p1, place marker, p9, place marker, p1, place marker, p7, k2.

Begin raglan increases and buttonholes

Row 1 (RS) With MC, k3, yo, k2tog, *knit to 1 stitch before the marker, kf&b, slip marker, k1, slip marker, kf&b; repeat from * 3 times, knit to the end of the row.
Row 2 (WS) K2, purl to the last 2 stitches, k2.
Row 3 With CC, k2, *knit to 1 stitch before the marker, kf&b, slip marker, k1, slip marker, kf&b, repeat from * 3 times, knit to the end of the row.
Row 4 Repeat **Row 2**.

Repeat these 4 rows 3 more times—122 stitches.

Create henley opening and join to work in the round

Slip the last 5 stitches from the end without buttonholes to a spare double-pointed or circular needle. These stitches will become the button band. Hold the piece to join in the round with the right side facing, overlapping the first and last 5 stitches so that the buttonholes are on top. Work the three-needle non-bind-off (page 12) over 3 stitches, place a different colored marker to note the beginning of the round; finish the non-bind-off over the next 2 stitches, and then continue knitting in the round as directed below.

Note: The join may create a small gap at the bottom edge of the button band. This can be sewn closed from the wrong side during finishing.

Continue raglan increases in the round

Round 1 (RS) *Knit to 1 stitch before the marker, kf&b, slip marker, k1, slip marker, kf&b; repeat from * 3 times, knit to the end of the round.
Round 2 Knit.

Repeat **Rounds 1 and 2** until the sleeve portion of the sweater measures 7" (18cm) across (measure between the increases). End with **Round 2**.

Place sleeve stitches on holders

On the next right-side row, knit to the 1st raglan marker, place the sleeve stitches (up to the 3rd marker) on holder, removing markers, cast on 2 stitches under the arm, knit across the back to the 6th marker, place the stitches for the 2nd sleeve on a holder (up to 8th marker), cast on 2 stitches under the arm, knit to the end of the round.

Work even in stockinette stitch for 6" (15cm).

Set-up to work the inseam

Count your stitches and place a removable marker or safety pin directly across from the beginning of round marker, dividing the stitches in half.

Continuing to follow the stripe sequence, and starting at the center front marker, k5, place marker, knit to 5 stitches before the 2nd marker, place marker, k5, remove center back marker, k5, place marker, knit to 5 stitches before the beginning of round marker, place marker, k5, remove beginning of round marker. There are 10 stitches marked at the center front and the center back.

INSEAM

The inseam is worked with short rows across the center front 10 stitches.
Row 1 From the beginning of round, k5 (to the marker), turn.
Row 2 s1, p9, turn.
Row 3 s1, k9, turn.

Repeat **Rows 2-3** until inseam piece measures 2½" (6.5cm)

Join the flap to the backside of the pajamas

With right sides together, and the wrong side facing, join the inseam flap to the center back 10 stitches using a three-needle bind-off. Fasten off.

LEGS

Place the stitches for the left leg on a stitch holder and continue working on the right leg only. With the right side facing, using circular or double-pointed needles, pick up and knit 12 stitches along the side of the inseam. Pick up and knit 2 stitches from the corner where the inseam meets the leg stitches, knit across the leg stitches, pick up 2 stitches from the corner where the leg stitches meet the inseam. Join and continue knitting in the round.
Work in stockinette stitch for 4" (10cm).

FORM FOOT

Round 1 *K1, k2tog, repeat from * around.
Rounds 2-4 Knit.

Repeat **Rounds 1-4** two more times. Break off yarn, thread end of yarn on a needle, and draw through remaining stitches. Pull closed.

Work the leg and the foot on the second side as for the first.

Make Custom-Sized PJs

1. Measure the back of the toy's neck and record that measurement here: _____ (N)

2. Record your gauge: _____ (G)

3. Multiply your gauge by your neck measurement: (G) x (N) = _____ (N1)

4. Take the result and multiply that by 2 to add sleeve stitches: (N1) x 2 = _____ (N2)

5. The raglan increases surround four "seam" stitches, which help to mark the increase and give a decorative look to the garment. These stitches need to be added to your cast-on. The result is your cast-on amount: (N2) + 4 = _____ (CO)

6. Calculate arm stitches: (N1) ÷ 2 = _____ (A)

7. Subtract your button band stitches from the arm stitches to get your front stitches: (A) - 2 = _____ (F)

Cast on according to your calculations and set up for raglan increases as follows:

Use your back neck stitch count (N1) as a guide for placing the markers.

Row 1 K2 (garter edge) k (F), place marker, k1, place marker, k (A), place marker, k1, place marker, k(N1), place marker, k1, place marker, k(A), place marker, k1, place marker, k(F), k2 (garter edge).

Follow the main pattern starting with **Begin raglan increases and buttonholes**.

Notes
Work the raglan increases until the arm portion of the sweater can wrap comfortably around your toy's arm. If you're knitting for a very small toy, you may want to work fewer buttonholes and a narrower inseam. Adjust the length of the arms, body, and legs according to your toy's measurements.

SLEEVES

Slip the stitches from the first sleeve back onto size 7 (4.5mm) needles. Knit across these stitches with MC, pick up and knit 2 stitches under the arm, and join to work in the round.
Work even in stockinette stitch (do not work stripe sequence) for 3" (7.5cm). Change to k1, p1 rib and work 6 rows. Bind off.

Repeat for the second sleeve.

FINISHING

Sew up any gaps. Sew on buttons. Weave in ends.

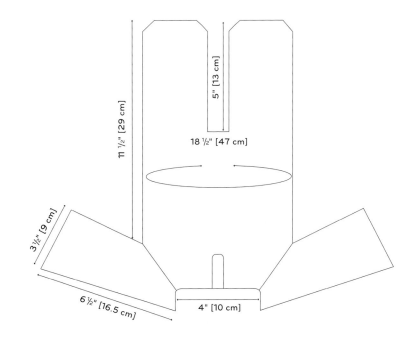

FUZZY WUZZY BATHROBE

Joey likes to be cozy before and after his soak in the tub, and what could be better than this fuzzy robe made from a luxurious cotton-bamboo bouclé yarn? The kimono-style robe is knit from hem to hem in one piece starting at the back bottom edge, with only a small bit of sewing to close the side and underarm seams.

Skill Level

Beginner

Finished Measurements

Chest Circumference: 22" (56cm)

Length: 10½" (26.5cm)

Sleeve: 5½" (14cm) from shoulder to cuff

Belt Length: 30" (76cm)

Materials

3 skeins Lily Chin Signature Collection Manhattan [87% California cotton, 13% bamboo; 71 yd (64m) per 1¾ oz (50g)], color: 135 (MC), (5) bulky

1 skein Lily Chin Signature Collection Manhattan [87% California cotton, 13% bamboo; 71 yd (64m) per 1¾ oz (50g)], color: 20 (CC), (5) bulky

Size 9 (5.5mm) circular needles, or size needed to obtain gauge

Sewing thread and needle

Measuring tape

Yarn needle

Stitch holder

Gauge

16 stitches and 32 rows = 4" (10 cm) in garter stitch

BODY

With CC, cast on 36 stitches.
Work in garter stitch for 1" (2.5cm).
Switch to MC, and work in garter stitch until piece measures 7" (18cm) from the cast-on edge, ending with a wrong-side row.

Add Sleeve stitches

Cast on 18 stitches with a cable cast-on. Knit across all 54 stitches, then, at the end of the row, cast on 18 stitches for the second sleeve—72 stitches.

Work in garter stitch across all stitches until your work measures 10½" (26.5cm) from the cast-on edge, ending with a right-side row.

Bind off neck stitches

On the next wrong-side row, k27, bind off 18 stitches, knit to the end of the row.

Slide stitches from the left side of the work onto a holder.

RIGHT SIDE NECK SHAPING

Row 1 (RS) Knit to 3 stitches before neck edge, kf&b, k2.
Row 2 (WS) Knit.

Repeat **Rows 1 and 2** until the sleeve measures 7" (18cm) from the sleeve cast-on. End with a wrong-side row.

Bind off sleeve stitches

Row 1 (RS) Bind off 18 stitches, knit to 3 stitches before the neck edge, kf&b, k2.
Row 2 Knit.

Continue to work **right side neck shaping Rows 1 and 2** until you have 36 stitches. Work even until the Right Front measures 9½" (24cm).

Switch to CC. Work in garter stitch for 1" (2.5cm). Bind off.

LEFT SIDE NECK SHAPING

Slip the stitches for the left side from the holder onto your needle. Join MC and work as for Right Side Neck Shaping, being sure to work increases at the neck edge.

With MC, cast on 6 stitches. Work 3" (7.5cm) in garter stitch. Switch to CC, and continue in garter stitch for 24" (61cm). Switch to MC. Work 3" (7.5cm) in garter stitch. Bind off.

CONTRASTING CUFFS

With CC, pick up stitches evenly along the first cuff. Work 1" (2.5cm) in garter stitch. Bind off. Repeat for the second cuff.

Fold the robe in half at the shoulders. Sew sleeve and side seams.

Weave in all ends.

Make a Custom-Sized Bathrobe

1. Measure the toy's circumference at its widest point: _____ (C)

2. Add 2" (5cm) of ease:
   (C) + 2 (5)= _____ (W)

3. Record your gauge: _____ (G)

4. Multiply your gauge by your adjusted circumference to get your cast-on:
   (G) x (W) = _____ (CO)

Cast on according to your calculations, and follow the instructions as written in the main pattern, noting the following changes.

Notes
- When you cast on for the sleeves, cast on half the number of stitches you used for the body on each side.

- When you bind off for the neck, measure the toy's neck, add 1" (2.5cm) of ease, and then multiply this number by your gauge. Bind off this number of stitches at the center of the piece.

- When you increase for the fronts, increase until each piece matches the number of stitches cast on for the back.

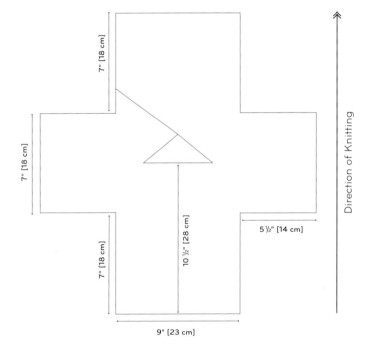

7" [18 cm]

7" [18 cm]

7" [18 cm]

10 ½" [28 cm]

5 ½" [14 cm]

9" [23 cm]

Direction of Knitting

Abbreviations

Here are the standard abbreviations used in the book. Project-specific abbreviations and special stitches are defined at the beginning of each pattern.

K	knit
P	purl
TOG	together
MM	millimeters
CM	centimeters
"	inches
WS	wrong side
SL	slip 1 (as in "slip 1 stitch")
PSSO	pass the slipped stitch(es) over
TBL	through the back loop of the stitch
YO	yarn over

SC	single crochet
DC	double crochet
CH	chain
K2TOG	(right-leaning decrease) knit two stitches together
SSK	(left-leaning decrease) slip 2 stitches, insert the left needle back into the stitches, and knit them together through the back loops.
M1	(increase) make one stitch by picking up the bar between two stitches and knitting into it.
KF&B	(increase) knit into the front of a stitch, then knit into the back of the same stitch

Sources and Resources

In choosing the yarns for this book, I paid special attention to fiber and color. These yarns are soft, durable, meant for play, and a joy to knit with. I also was interested in yarns that are ecologically produced as well as yarns manufactured using socially responsible practices. You'll find more information about the yarns and where to get them at the manufacturers' websites or by contacting them directly.

ALCHEMY YARNS OF TRANSFORMATION
www.alchemyyarns.com

BE SWEET
www.besweetproducts.com

BERNAT
www.bernat.com

BROWN SHEEP
www.brownsheep.com

ELMORE PISGAH
www.elmore-pisgah.com

JOSEPH GALLER YARNS
5 Mercury Avenue,
Monroe, NY 10950
800-836-3314

KNIT ONE, CROCHET TOO
www.knitonecrochettoo.com

LILY CHIN SIGNATURE
COLLECTION BY CNS YARNS
www.lilychinsignaturecollection.com

LION BRAND
www.lionbrand.com

NATURE'S PALETTE
www.handjiveknits.com

SOUTH WEST TRADING COMPANY
www.soysilk.com

TILLI TOMAS
www.tillitomas.com

VERMONT ORGANIC FIBER CO.
www.vtorganicfiber.com

General Guidelines for Yarn Weights

The Craft Yarn Council of America has instituted a number system for knitting and crochet yarn gauges and recommended needle and hook sizes. The information provided below is intended as a guideline, and as always, swatching is key to being sure a chosen yarn is a good match for the intended project. More information can be found at www.yarnstandards.com.

CYCA	1 SUPER FINE	2 FINE	3 LIGHT	4 MEDIUM	5 BULKY
Yarn Weight	Lace, Fingering, Sock	Sport	DK, Light Worsted	Worsted, Aran	Chunky
Avg. Knitted Gauge over 4" (10cm)	27–32 sts	23–26 sts	21–24 sts	16–20 sts	12–15 sts
Recommended Needle in US Size Range	1–3	3–5	5–7	7–9	9–11
Recommended Needle in Metric Size Range	2.25–3.25mm	3.25–3.75mm	3.75–4.5mm	4.5–5.5mm	5.5–8mm

*Guidelines Only: The above reflect the most commonly used gauges and needle or hook sizes for specific yarn categories.

Acknowledgments

This project was a tremendous group effort and I'm grateful to everyone involved. When I learned I was going to be creating over 20 itty-bitty garments in the space of a couple of months, I knew I needed reinforcements. I offered the knitting "opportunity" to the lively and creative Silver Spring Knitters group, my local social weekly knitting gathering. Thanks to Martha Hulse for starting "SSK" and taking me in when I was new to the area. Those instant friendships have turned into lasting and dear ones.

Five members of SSK had their hands in this book and I can't thank them enough. Thank you so much to Hillary Catlin, who proved she's not only an expert knitter, but can think like a designer; to Lisa Chaki, who went from knitting her first project ever to knitting the Fuzzy Wuzzy Bathrobe in what seemed like a few short weeks; to Michelle Embry and Hannah Joyner for their expert interpretation of my designer's shorthand. Thank you to Jennifer Woods, who not only knit two of my designs, but designed the amazing Fair Isle sweater. Thanks also to Jennifer—who, when she's not knitting, is a first-class graphic designer—for creating all of the technical art for the book.

Thank you to all of the yarn companies who donated materials for the projects in this book: Alchemy Yarns of Transformation, Be Sweet, Knit One Crochet Too, Lily Chin Signature Collection, Nature's Palette, Southwest Trading Company, Tilli Tomas, and Vermont Organics.

Thank you to Kristi Porter for her keen eye in technical editing as well as her advice and friendship. Thank you to my editors at Potter Craft, Melissa Bonventre and Courtney Conroy for their encouragement and confidence.

Finally, thank you to my family—my mom, dad, and brother, who are a constant support in all I do; to my children, Jay and Selma, who provided inspiration and feedback about the projects; and to my husband James, for helping to keep me on task and for his support and love throughout the project.

Index